JOHN F

# RIDING
## WITH GHOSTS,
## ANGELS,
## AND THE
## SPIRITS
## OF THE DEAD

outskirts
press

# Table of Contents

# Dedication

TO ALL OF my guys on the Other Side: those spirits, angels, beings, and guides who have painstakingly watched over me, guided me, helped me, rescued me, and yes, who have literally saved my life many times. Thank you!

To the Old Black Ghost: I hope you found your way. Message received, and hopefully, delivered.

To my family.

To my dad, who came in spirit to view my painting.

To my old buddy Bill Nunn, who sometimes visits me in dreams from the Other Side. To Jim Cogan; he's the one who knows. To Lee Williams; ride on, Cowboy! To William "Smituska" Smith; confidant and drinking buddy.

To Eric Huber, the best riding buddy a guy ever had.

To Jim Mullen, my friend and my TV producer. Thanks, old chum.

To all of my friends who have been a blessing to my life over the years.

To all of the fur babies who have graced my life with their love, especially Skeezix and Bugsy.

To my sweet Melissa, for the 113,000+ miles of adventures (and counting).

To Julie, whose bark is not nearly as bad as her bite.

And to Marjorie, for choosing to love me and to rescue me and to enjoy with me: Life, both seen and unseen.

# Introduction

I'VE BEEN A professional psychic for over 45 years; and a biker for over 50. After several decades of life as a psychic and paranormal investigator, and with many miles spent in the saddles of my motorcycles, my psychic gift–along with my penchant for attracting bizarre otherworldly encounters–and my love of motorcycling merged and the result is these stories of psychic and paranormal adventures that are truly unique in the realm of spiritual literature.

This collection of supernatural experiences from the road are necessarily episodic: you can't make an appointment with a UFO; the paranormal is by nature seemingly fickle and most of the time you take what you can get, when you can get it. There's not a continuum to be found but rather we learn that the Other Side presents itself to us in a peek-a-boo manner: most paranormal experiences are isolated episodes that stand alone with a distinct lesson to learn from each individual event. Consider my book as a collection of true ghost stories, each with its own merit and food for thought.

The common bond–or story arc, if you will–is my motorcycle; think: *Then Came Bronson* meets the supernatural.

Come along with me and enjoy the ride.

John Russell

# Funereal Aethereal

WHILE MY WIFE and I were enjoying life in upstate New York I was contacted by multiple award-winning producer Jim Mullen–who at the time was working for Atlas Media in New York City–to shoot a TV pilot for The History Channel.

The pilot episode focused on my psychic investigation into the assassination of President Abraham Lincoln and the subsequent search for his notorious killer, John Wilkes Booth.

While all of us–me, Jim, and the crew–considered the pilot to be a smashing success, there was one thing that I couldn't satisfactorily obtain either psychically or through normal channels: the knowledge of the whereabouts of Lincoln's funeral hearse. It became an *obsession* with me, and I couldn't figure out why.

I asked Jim about the hearse; he didn't know. I think I may have asked a few other people; they didn't know either. At the time that frustrated me immensely: For some oddball reason finding out the then current whereabouts of Lincoln's funeral hearse became a preoccupation with me. Over the years I've learned that most of the time when I begin to experience something like that I eventually realize, at some point, that I'm obsessing about something because the Other Side *wants* me to: the obsession, if properly followed up on and explored, will lead to further revelations or information that is useful either for me, my clients, or both. But while filming the pilot I ran up against a dead end regarding the hearse and as time went by I began to think less and less about it, although it would periodically reenter my mind. Psychically, for me, it remained a loose end. I had *wanted* to find that hearse! I had wanted to stand before it and allow its energies to flow into me, to receive the impressions from Lincoln's funeral procession. For me it felt like it would have been a *vital* part of my psychic investigation, one more piece of the puzzle falling into place. But alas it was not to be; we wrapped up filming without ever learning the whereabouts of the hearse.

Well, maybe some things aren't meant to be.

Years later, a thousand miles away, and one new motorcycle

Buy American. (I agree.) Buy a Harley. Even though they have become increasingly metric and even though many of their parts are farmed out for overseas manufacture now, for the most part I can agree.

Although I bought a Honda. People love to bash Hondas: they're Japanese, and those damn Japs attacked us without provocation at Pearl Harbor. True, and true. But not every Japanese person hated, or hates, America, and I'm sure many of them were against the war.

And at the time I bought my Honda they had a manufacturing plant here in the good old U.S. of A, providing Americans with jobs.

I first went to a Harley-Davidson dealership to buy a Harley. After standing around for a good bit of time drooling over the machines while every sales person ignored me like the plague I went and bought myself a new Honda instead.

Black. Purty. 1300cc engine; 80 cubic inches. Plenty of power to haul me and my gear around the highways. Not a mile on her. She told me her name was Melissa. I fell in love.

To date we've ridden over 113,500 miles together; we've gotten to know each other pretty well, and we've had some fabulous adventures. But a funny thing begin to happen on some of our rides: the Other Side begin to provide some pretty astonishing supernatural manifestations, and I don't believe that I would have experienced these things in quite the ways that I would have if I had been covering the same miles in a car.

There's something about being on a bike that connects you with the road, the air, the countryside, the weather, the sunshine and clouds and rain, the heat and the cold, and even the spiritual realm like nothing else does. The feeling produced borders on the ecstatic. Throw in some spooky stuff courtesy of the Other Side and you've got some real adventures, my friend! Such as my journey to Tallahassee...

For a few days now I've been having psychic impulses to ride to Tallahassee, Florida's state capital. I periodically feel a sense of urgency to get on the road, with the particular destination being Tallahassee.

I don't know why I'm receiving these psychic prompts, but they're increasing in frequency and intensity, and while the Other Side urges me to ride to Tallahassee they don't tell me why, but I know that there has got to be a particular reason and I hope that I can discover it easily when I arrive there.

Do you ever feel like you're supposed to do a certain thing, perform a certain action, or travel to a certain place or destination, but you're not quite sure why? Yeah, me too. And sometimes the purpose of a trip will smack me in the face as soon as I get to my destination, and then at other times I have to do a bit of psychic detective work before things finally fall into place and begin to make sense for me.

I'm hoping that the Other Side will reveal why it is that they're urging me to ride to Tallahassee, but so far they have not, so today, as my urgings have peaked in intensity, I have scheduled myself a day off from giving psychic readings for my worldwide clientele. I have woken up early as is my custom and I unfold and check my map: I'm to take I-10 west. Tallahassee is within easy striking distance for a day's roundtrip ride of between 450-500 miles, a distance that I'm used to covering comfortably in a day on my motorcycle.

The weather forecast promises blue skies and sunshine and lots of

Florida's infamous heat, so I fill my new Th_____
ter and stash it in one of my saddlebags, _____
are plenty of good rest stops with water an_____
worry about staying hydrated.

My throttle hand is always itching: eve_____
motorcycle at a young age I have relished _____
ever made on a bike, whether it was a shor_ ___p or a few blocks to
pick up a few items at the grocery store or an all-day ride of hundreds
of miles or, even better, an overnight journey.

So I finish packing a few additional items onto Melissa, my faithful bike, check her fluids and tire pressures, and make sure that all of
her lights and signals are in good working order, and I hit the road,
eager not only to discover the purpose and meaning of this paranormal nudge to ride to Tallahassee but I'm also delighted to be able to
once again put this many miles on my faithful iron horse. Ever since
I was a kid, motion– movement–has been important to me: it's both
an escape and a therapy, and I used to beg my parents to take me for
rides in their car. I couldn't wait until I was old enough to be able to
venture out on my own, and I spent many happy days in my youth
driving my own car and riding my motorcycles on highways and by-
ways for hours and hours at a time, a true nomad at heart.

And now that I'm able to roam about as I please I take full advan-
tage of it: it's not unusual for me to rise before 6 a.m., fire up the bike,
ride from Florida to Savannah, Georgia, see a few sights, stop and eat
a hamburger, and then ride back home, covering between 450-500
plus miles in the process. So Tallahassee? Ha…no step for a stepper.

And what a gorgeous day for my journey: blue skies, sunshine,
and the sweet song of Melissa's powerful motor humming as we fly
down the highway, knowing only our destination but not our purpose. What a grand adventure!

My trip on I-10 west is so far pleasurable and uneventful…until
I hit a traffic jam; a *large* traffic jam that sits dead still. I put my kickstand down, turn off my bike and dismount, and I walk over to the
median so that I can look far down the straight, flat highway and try

to determine why we're stuck. Up ahead I can see a major wreck and both I-10 east and I-10 west are closed. *Damn.*

Not only do I have concerns for those involved in the accident, but the thought crosses my mind that my trip to our state's capital will have to be postponed and that I will probably have to turn around and take a different ride today, and I wonder if I do so if I will lose contact with the particular purpose that the Other Side has in sending me to Tallahassee this day? What if the future timing is wrong and this particular psychic urge never returns, or what if it does but I'm somehow out of sync with things when I arrive and then I never can figure out why the Powers That Be are prompting me to take this ride? It's frustrating to me to have these thoughts, and a little unsettling to think that I might be forced to miss out on something important.

But then I have a sudden feeling that I should take out my hand-held CB radio and see if those who are close to the wreck can tell me what's going on and approximately how long our delay will be. Maybe I will be able to fulfill my destiny today after all.

I turn on my CB and *Sweet merciful crap,* as Homer Simpson would say!

I used to use CB radio with some regularity when I was in my mid to late teens and early 20s but I haven't been on the air for over 30 years now and when I switch on channel 19 to try and get some information from either the truckers who are close to the accident or anyone else up there who might have a CB, I'm astonished: the barrage of juvenile cursing, filthy chatter, and off-color remarks takes even me aback, and that's saying something.

I'm far from being a prude, and my old lady says that sailors should come to me to learn how to curse, but what I'm hearing is something else...silly mindless filth and sexual slurs that are so juvenile and vile that they don't even deserve the lofty connotation of ribaldry, and all of this mindless chatter is driven with an energy of pure aggression and absolutely no compassion.

I had expected to tune into the CB airwaves of my youth and to be greeted by polite chatter and then to be able to obtain some useful information that will help me to make an informed decision about whether or not to continue my trip, but this obviously ain't my daddy's CB radio anymore. I am literally repulsed.

The useless chatter pouring forth from my CB radio (One trucker: "See that woman standing by the blue car? Maybe the wind will blow her dress up and I'll at least have a good view of something while I'm sitting here waiting.") is so incessant that I can't even get a word in edgewise to ask for a "break" and then try to find out what's going on.

I continue to listen and in amongst the ruthless nonstop chatter I manage to hear someone who is right on top of the scene of the accident say that a Life Flight helicopter is coming to evacuate one of the victims of the wreck; that can't be good. I say a silent prayer for the poor person who is to be evacuated by helicopter and I continue to listen to the chatter.

One of the truckers makes the heartless remark that he wishes they'd hurry up and get the person out of the way then so that he could get back on the road! I wonder what he would feel in his heart if that was his wife lying there waiting to be evacuated by helicopter to a hospital where they would try and save her life and he overheard others saying that they wish to hell they'd get on with it then and get her out of the way so that they could continue on their trip. Whatever happened to common courtesy? Is this who we've become? Have compassion and empathy become so meaningless in our lives? My feelings are hurt by this barrage of self-centered claptrap.

I see the Life Flight helicopter arrive, and then after a long interval it takes off again and I hear someone on the CB say that they're about to reopen I-10 west so I repack my CB, put my helmet back on and remount my bike, and soon we're moving once again. I hope, among all of my other fellow travelers, that I'm not the only one that has said a prayer for the accident victims.

And I'm still shocked and dismayed by the drivel that has poured out of my CB radio, and for the next several miles of my trip I mull over man's inhumanity to man, aware that the questions that I have are those that men wiser than I am have wrestled with since time began, and we seem to be no closer to meaningful solutions. I feel a little sad in spite of having these miles and miles to cover, which for me is normally one of the most pleasurable sensations that I know.

But then–so typical of we easily distracted human beings (Is it any wonder we have difficulties achieving spiritual enlightenment?)–farther down the road I cross the famed Suwannee River and now for the next several miles I can't get the song lyrics out of my head.

*Way down upon the Swanee River,*
*Far, far away.*
*That's where my heart is yearning ever,*
*Home where the old folks stay.*

The lyrics and the melody won't go away and so I begin to sing them to myself over and over in my mind, and at one point I actually burst out loud into song, filling my helmet with my voice's reverberations and then I begin to laugh out loud at myself.

At least I'm not thinking about the drivel from my CB radio anymore.

Seems like we have to spend a lot of our time distracting ourselves from the ugliness of life, doesn't it? Like I've done just now. That's why we attend plays, go to movies, read books, watch TV…and ride motorcycles: to connect with something that reveals some of the beauty of life and reminds us of what it could be like if we would all focus on these pleasurable joys instead of thinking up more creative ways to torture and harm and kill each other.

After many more, thankfully, uneventful miles turned pleasurable again I'm getting close to my destination of our state's capital when I see a sign advertising the Tallahassee Automobile Museum, and I get that peculiar but familiar blip on my psychic radar screen that suddenly lets me know that *this museum* is my destination today, and not Tallahassee proper. Hmm. This I don't understand *at all:* I'm a bike guy, not a car guy, although I do have an appreciation for hot rods and antique automobiles. But an *auto museum?* The Other Side has prompted me to ride all these many miles to bring me to an auto museum? What happened to Tallahassee? Have I misunderstood the guidance I've received from the Other Side? This makes no sense to me whatsoever but over the years I've learned to trust and obey my psychic promptings and so I pull into the parking lot.

I turn Melissa off and dismount, taking in the lay of the land as I pull off my gloves and my helmet. There's some beautiful landscaping here, and the place has a good energy, a good feel to it. The day's still bright and beautiful and sunny and my good mood has returned in full force, although I'm still confused as to why the Other Side has led me to this auto museum instead of having me continue my journey into Tallahassee proper.

I straighten up and stretch and I glance around at the earth and the sky and I'm filled with admiration for the beauty of nature that I'm allowed to experience this day. And then, just as I finish locking up my bike, a pair of geese flies close by me on a long, low, level flight; they're only a few feet off the ground. I believe that they're the first geese I've seen since I've moved to Florida. I feel a brief pang in my heart: I suddenly miss New York.

I *loved* living there, upstate in the mountains, where one of my favorite things to do was to watch the geese flying, the scene reminiscent of the paintings that graced the pages of the West Texas drug store calendars I used to gaze on when I was a boy, and I used to wonder way back then if such sentimental sights really existed somewhere, or were they just the figment of some artist's imagination?

Once while living in New York I remember I was outside working in my yard and it was chilly and the sky was overcast. I heard one faint, distant, almost plaintive honk and looked up to see a large v-formation of geese flying high overhead and as I watched them they literally flew into the clouds and disappeared from view.

The sight made such an impression on me that my heart actually leapt when I saw it. For all of the despair and ugliness in this old world, it sure contains a lot of grace and beauty too, doesn't it? It's one of those strange dichotomies of Life that we all have to wrestle with and try to somehow make sense out of, either by developing a theology of our own to explain it, or adopting someone else's.

And now, today, standing in this faraway parking lot in Florida beside my beloved Melissa the incongruity of these geese blasting by me in the heat of this sunshiny day forcibly brings that autumnal memory back to me and I'm suddenly in a *New York State of Mind,* if you please, Mr. Joel.

And then I get another feeling; a psychic feeling: these geese seem to be a portent. But of what are they an omen? I feel like something significant is just on the horizon, but what? And whatever it is it must surely occur elsewhere on this day's journey, because what could possibly happen that's of any great psychic portent at an automotive museum?

As I walk across the parking lot for no reason I suddenly start thinking about filming my psychic investigation of Lincoln's assassination and now all of a sudden, out of the blue, those memories come flooding back to me too as I enter the museum. What a strange day this is turning out to be!

I pay my admission fee and then I begin to look around. It is an automobile museum alright, as advertised, and here on the main floor there are lots of hot rods and antique cars, but the museum has two floors and there are also tons of other neat things to look at and enjoy: sports memorabilia; old ornate slot machines; a collection of outboard boat motors; a huge collection of pocket knives, and much, much more. What a wonderful and fascinating place. I'm happy to be here; I'm enjoying the visit so far, but I'm still confused as to why I was led here in the first place.

But it doesn't take me but a moment longer to find out. Before I've even begun to browse the whole first floor of this museum, much less make it up to the second floor, there is a vehicle that catches my eye from across the room. My psychic senses immediately go on full alert and without even reading the sign that describes it I know what this vehicle is, and I know it's why the Other Side has led me here today.

But I don't hurry to make my way to it. Instead I *savor* the discovery, and I occasionally allow myself to glance in its direction as I look at the other treasures in the museum while I continue to walk toward it.

And then I'm standing before it. It's an old, horse drawn hearse. The sign says that it's *the funeral hearse that hauled President Abraham Lincoln's body.* Man, I've got goose bumps! My feet are frozen to the spot, and I have to consciously check to make sure that my mouth isn't agape. When I can gather my wits I actually look around the museum to see if the ghost of Mr. Lincoln is standing somewhere and staring at me, and smiling. If he is, I don't see him, and for some reason that makes me feel a little wistful. I wish that I knew that he was here to celebrate this powerful moment with me.

I'm so powerfully overawed to be experiencing this physical evidence that across the years and across the miles something, someone, has guided me to this place and to this hearse, which was the object of my obsession when I was a thousand miles and many years away from here.

I give my thanks to the Other Side, and to the spirit of President Lincoln, and after standing before this delightful object a few reverential moments longer I allow myself to enjoy exploring the rest of the museum. But before I leave I make sure that I come and stand before Lincoln's hearse and pay tribute one more time to his memory, and to give thanks to the Powers That Be that were able to influence me to make this trip in order that I could experience this sweet closure and to find out the answer to my question with which I was so obsessed so many years ago in Washington, DC: "Does anybody know the whereabouts of the funeral hearse that carried Lincoln's body?"

Well, yes...*someone* knew; they knew it all along. It just took a few years and a move across the country and this ride today of a little over 200 miles to connect me to it. The time had to be right. All of the conditions had to come together to make, for me, this to be one of the most delightful and memorable psychic experiences I've ever had.

It also, for me, makes a wonderful closure to that paranormal investigation of years ago, and satisfies me in ways that are hard to even try to explain.

Think how astonishing this experience is, and the powerful life lessons we can learn from it.

Why, so long ago and so many miles away in our nation's capital, as I psychically investigated Lincoln's assassination, did powerful spiritual forces influence me to become obsessed with finding Lincoln's funeral hearse?

I believe that the reason was so that I could have reinforced for me in a powerfully dramatic way a lesson that I already knew: In truth there are powerful, unseen forces that are aware of even the most minute details of what goes on in our earthly lives, and they can guide us to revelations, understandings, and solutions...even if it takes a journey of many years and a thousand miles to do so. And so that I could share this truth, and this journey, this moment...with you. I hope it inspires you as it has me.

Does this mean that every inquiry or request that we make of the Other Side will be met with an answer, or an understanding, or an eventual resolution or solution? No.

Why not? I don't know why, and I believe that anyone who tells you that they do know or that they have the answers is self-deluded and lying to you, because Life *is* a mystery, a Great Unknown for which theologians and metaphysicians and wise men and dreamers and artists and scholars have all sought out solutions and answers and reasons why. And have most times been sorely disappointed.

It seems like this Life is set up that way–for whatever reasons–and that sometimes we are blessed to find the answers that we seek, and yet at other times we stumble onward while cursing the darkness and our little candle burns away without shining nearly enough light into the gloom–literal and metaphorical–that surrounds us.

I mentioned to you earlier that I've had over 800 paranormal experiences in my life so far. These are real experiences that have actually occurred on the physical plane, not things that I have dreamed, saw in a vision of some sort, or hallucinated, and many times I, and others, have caught them on film or video, or recorded them on audio, or others have witnessed them with their own eyes. I have been blessed to interact with the Other Side since I was a small child, and these experiences have taught me much; they have also left me scratching my head and wondering, *why?*

And perhaps that's the true meaning of Faith, in the most absolute sense of the word: that we are to walk in whatever amount of light that we're given in spite of the questions and worries and fears that we have, and in spite of the unanswered prayers and incomplete answers that we continue to seek more light, and enlightenment, while nonetheless continuing to hold fast to a resolve to do good unto others for goodness own sake, and hoping and believing that will be its own reward...and ours.

And realizing that every now and then the Other Side throws us a pretty large bone. And that an expression of gratitude is in order when we receive such a precious gift.

We won't understand it all, but we can understand some of it, and in the process we can do all of the good that we can for ourselves and for others, and maybe, just maybe, we'll gain more understanding when we get to whatever the Other Side is.

In the meantime experiences such as this one are pretty powerful and eye-opening, and are to be treasured and mulled over. I think that there may be many more lessons to be gleaned from this one dramatic experience; what do you think? What insights can you gain into your own life from my experience? Does it cause you to question and reevaluate your own beliefs and choices? Or perhaps it reinforces for you, in a comforting way, that we are indeed looked out for and watched over, although in ways that may seem to us to be incomplete or imperfect at the time. What are your thoughts?

I hope you've enjoyed riding along with me on this fascinating journey. But our time here at this intriguing place is over. Let's saddle up...we have hundreds more miles to cover and some more incredibly amazing things to experience. Life is full of wonder if we'll just take the time to look and listen. Let's go see what else we can find!

## Epilogue

For the next several weeks I find an *abnormal* amount of Lincoln pennies *everywhere;* I *see* the name "Lincoln" frequently, excessively; and there is an abundance of Abraham Lincoln memorabilia and related items that I encounter at every turn and in the most unlikely of places. It refreshes my memories of what was surely one of the most unique paranormal investigations I've ever conducted. As well as one of the most unique rides I've ever taken. And it lets me know that the Other Side continues to watch over me and to communicate with me, and to be considerate of things that I hold to be important.

And...that I'm not supposed to forget this tremendous experience. Neither are you, yours.

CHAPTER **II**

# Going Bananas

I'M SOUND ASLEEP in my home in Florida, and I'm aware that I'm having a lucid dream (a lucid dream is any dream in which one is *aware* that one is dreaming). I decide to not try and control the dream but to just go with it and see where it takes me because the experience, so far at least, is a very pleasurable one because in it I'm riding my motorcycle.

I've owned a few motorcycles in my life, starting around the age of 15 when I first became a biker, but I've never ridden *any* of them in my dreams...until now; in this dream I am riding my latest motorcycle, a Honda VTX 1300C, which is a big, black, shiny, fast, powerful, throbbing v-twin named Melissa. I know that is her name, because when we first met she told me so.

My dream is so real that I can feel myself sitting in the low-slung leather seat of my motorcycle; I can literally feel myself holding onto the handlebars; and I can feel the wind in my face as I ride down the road. In my dream these sensations are every bit as real and pleasurable as they are in my waking state and I'm enjoying them immensely.

As my dream progresses I notice that I'm riding down a long, straight two-lane country road, as is often my habit in my waking state; Florida has a lot of them. There is no other traffic; I am alone on the road. Sometimes that's not too unusual for Florida back roads either.

The scenery is pleasant but mostly unremarkable, as is the scenery alongside many of these typical Florida backcountry roads: some pine woods here and there, some smaller trees of varying types, some scrub brush and saw palmetto, all disrupted by the periodic breaks in the trees and vegetation which allows me to see flat farmland, ranchland, or undeveloped acres of land. An occasional house here and there. Some horses or cattle grazing. I describe it as unremarkable, but in reality it's uncommonly beautiful to me, and I'm enjoying watching it as I glide along effortlessly on my powerful machine. *What a great dream.*

Up ahead on the right-hand side of the road I see a familiar sight: a green rectangular city limit sign. It's just a small, ordinary, nondescript city limit sign like those I regularly encounter when I'm entering some small Florida town or another but for some reason this particular sign really piques my interest. I begin to get a tingle of anticipation and I can't wait to see what it reads. It seems important to me that I should notice this sign and pay careful attention to it, so I begin to slow Melissa slightly as I approach the sign so that I can read it.

Now I'm close enough to the sign that I can see it clearly and the town's name to which the sign is welcoming me reads..."Banana."

I stop alongside the shoulder of the road before I pass the sign, and as Melissa quietly idles I sit on her staring at the city limit sign. It's taking a little time for this to sink in. *Banana.* And then I begin to laugh.

I shake my head. "Banana," I mutter.

*Okay, yes,* I think to myself in my dream, *I live in Florida now.* The word *banana* connotes the semi-tropical and tropical environments I have come to know and love in this state. Carrying the word association game further, banana trees even grow in the city in which I live, and a couple of my neighbors have them growing in their yards. I also remember that in some of the Florida state parks that I frequent I've seen bananas growing on the banana trees, in the wild. And I happen to love bananas as a food item...give me a good banana split and I'm in food heaven.

15

In my dream I bring my thoughts up short. Yes, all of the things that I've realized in association with this word are true, but my lord; what a bizarre thing to put into this dream. Why would I have a lucid dream in which I ride my motorcycle for miles down an empty road only to come to a town in Florida with a cliché for a name, and with no apparent meaning or significance beyond the trivial and the obvious?

*Banana*. Again, why such a powerful lucid dream in which I can literally experience it with all five of my physical senses that has only led me to a sign emblazoned with a cliché in the middle of nowhere? I smirk, and then I shift Melissa back into gear, and again I shake my head as I pass by the city limit sign. Banana indeed. In my mind the experience has taken on a very sophomoric tone because the Other Side (I'm assuming) chooses to convey to me, through such a simple and clichéd association, facts with which I'm already well aware. Hey, guys: I'm fully aware that I live, work, and play in this beautiful state of Florida...and as I'm thinking these thoughts as I'm accelerating Melissa to go on down the road I glance once again to the right-hand side of the road and I'm suddenly seeing tombstones. There are small tombstones, and medium-sized and large tombstones; some are ornate, some are very plain, and most of them are very old, weathered, and worn. They stretch for a short little distance down the highway before normal scenery resumes again, and about midway along this stretch of tombstones I stop Melissa, shut her off, dismount and walk over to inspect these old grave markers, many of which date back into the 1800s, and I think to myself that if the town of Banana, Florida ever did indeed exist it must have long ago faded away because it looks to me like all of its inhabitants are deceased.

Wow...what a puzzling dream this is turning into. Why would the Other Side show me all of these old tombstones in what has to be an imaginary town that apparently is no longer even in existence in its own dream? Maybe the Other Side is not communicating any great truths to me at all: maybe my dream is the result of my brain working overtime to sort out some problem in its own peculiar language and symbology. By now, who knows?

I mount up and ride Melissa farther down the road and there I encounter a small town, and this small town somehow seems to be either the remnants of Banana or a latter day version thereof, perhaps a community that grew up out of Banana's demise.

While I'm there I encounter an old friend from Texas (where I grew up and spent most of the years of my life), and we go into what seems to be a little café of sorts and we sit down at a table together and we talk over old times. But the reunion is disturbed by a murky undertone: it seems that he has something important that he wants to convey to me, or perhaps it's I who has something important to convey to him, but somehow, for whatever reasons, we both seem to be unable to articulate the information during our brief visit.

I rise from our table to leave, and I tell my old friend that it's sure been good to see him and that I hope that I'll get to see him again before too long. He wishes me well and I mount Melissa and fire her up and begin to ride out of this small town and then, abruptly, the dream comes to an end, and I pop up in bed, suddenly wide awake.

I sit in the darkness for a moment, listening to the gentle breathing of Marjorie as she lies asleep beside me. I replay the dream in my mind, trying to sort it out and make any sense of it. What message, what meaning is being conveyed? I can find none, so I quietly snort, shake my head and mutter *"Banana!"* And then I settle down and drift back off to sleep.

## The Next Morning: Saturday, August 29, 2009

As soon as we're both awake I relate my dream to Marjorie. She agrees with me that it seems to be very odd and very interesting, but it doesn't hold any special significance for her either. Neither one of us can figure out what the dream *means*. Was it one of those crazy random dreams which neither make sense as it's happening nor afterward? Or, was it some type of real communication, containing verifiable information that I should heed and on which I should follow up?

"Wouldn't it be something, though, if it turns out that there really is a Banana, Florida?" I ask her.

We both agree that it would indeed be something, but she reminds me that given the clichéd and somewhat seemingly frivolous Floridian name of the town in my dream that it's a real long shot that it could exist in reality.

"Still, just for grins I think I'm going to look on the Internet and see if anything pops up," I say, and I hop out of bed and cross our home and enter the room that serves as my office.

I go to Google's search page and type in "Banana, Florida," and hit Enter on my keyboard.

Oh...my...god. My mouth is hanging open.

First rattle out of the box up pops two links, for...Banana, Florida.

There is a very brief reference on Wikipedia which really doesn't tell me a whole lot, but then I find a map of old Banana which is now the town of Melrose; that's roughly about an hour away, what I consider to be a short hop on the bike.

I'm going to ride there, *right now,* because, incredibly, something or someone from the realm of spirit has given me concrete, verifiable information in my dream last night. I know that this must have real significance and I feel obligated to explore it further. So I'll head to the town of Melrose, not knowing what to expect, or what I'll find, or what I'll do when I get there. I have the vague notion that I'll just cruise around on my motorcycle and let my psychic senses guide me, and hopefully I'll be enough in tune with the Powers That Be that I will discover something interesting, or at least get the next piece of the puzzle that will help me to make sense of this dream that is a communication of some sort from the Other Side.

I get dressed, tell the Beloved goodbye as she wishes me luck in my psychic quest, and I warm Melissa up in anticipation of our ride. I mentally send out a signal to the Other Side to let them know that I have received their communication, that I'm following up on it, and that right now I'm heading to Melrose, where I hope that they will interact with me and explain to me what I am supposed to do with this knowledge that I've received.

I'm about to head to Banana, but I get lost in a moment of reverie as I throw my leg over Melissa and thumb the starter button. I didn't dream about Melissa before I met her, but I did have a bit of precognition about her...I knew that my next motorcycle (and possibly last: I tend to keep bikes a long time) would be a dark machine, dark in more senses of the word than just black in color; that she would be a machine possessed of a spirit of daring and adventure that would be a match for mine. Think of the aggressive, reckless, brave and courageous black mare as she rears up with might and power to assert her independence, power, and freedom, and you've got the right mental picture that floated through my mind in anticipation of my next two-wheeled ride.

And when we moved from New York to Florida I met her. She was a 2004 model that had been basically sitting on the showroom floor for a year, waiting on me to come along and rescue her and to get her on the road, where she craved to be.

I bought her brand spanking new without a mile on her and in four years we traveled over 70,000 miles together...all of that without an overnight trip. We've grown to know each other pretty well.

She'll still shine up like a brand new dime, and she runs like a scalded-ass ape, and on any given day at any given moment she is sufficiently maintained and packed with all of the essentials that I need to take off at a moment's notice on an extended road trip of any length and duration. She's a true road machine; a pleasure and a dream come true.

There's not too much that I can think of that I enjoy as much as riding her. It's fun! And one of the awesome side effects of riding her is that at some point during the trip all of the cobwebs in my brain just blow away with the wind and I'm totally relaxed and clearheaded, completely at one with the ride. Forty-five miles down the road this morning that effect occurs and I don't even think about Banana anymore, or the dream, or its possible meanings...I just tune into the marvelous feeling of speed experienced on two wheels as Melissa's powerful v-twin motor pulls me along effortlessly. I don't think a talented choir singing is as beautiful as the hum of that engine at speed and the windblast ripping at my helmeted ears as it competes for attention. I sure hope they have motorcycles on the Other Side.

After about an hour's pleasant journey I have arrived in Melrose, née Banana. I cruise straight through the Historic District hoping for a hint of Banana's past. Melrose's Historic District is all of a few blocks long and before I know it I'm riding out of town. Hmm. Well, what to do now? My psychic inspiration kicks in and I take a county road and I immediately feel like I'm heading in the right direction but that perhaps I'm too far over. Before long I feel compelled to turn off on another county road which leads me away from where I should be going, but I'm momentarily glad that I've taken this detour: there's a fantastic photo opportunity along the practically deserted road, an old building of some kind that burned down long ago, with a tall chimney still standing among the charred remains. I pull Melissa over and I take a few photos and then I continue onward, and before I know it I'm back on the main road which will take me back into Melrose, but coming into town from the opposite direction from which I originally traveled, and I'll make that same brief trek through the Historic District again.

I notice that there's a historical marker in front of a bank, and I brake and turn into the driveway going the wrong way, against the exit, but there's no traffic in the parking lot on this Saturday morning and I stop to read the sign, hoping that it'll tell me something about Banana. Nope: nothing.

I pull out of the parking lot and continue on down to another road and I feel like I should turn right, so I do, and I'm heading in the same direction that I felt was correct earlier, except that now I'm several blocks over, and it doesn't take me but a moment to realize that I'm now exactly where I'm supposed to be.

For I'm riding along on a stretch of flat, straight, two-lane road, that's still relatively backcountry in feel. Just as I was in my dream.

And then I spy it...on the right-hand side of the road sits a cemetery, and the gravestones are sitting about the same distance from the road as they were in my dream, and also, as in my dream, there are some small tombstones, and medium-sized and large tombstones, and some are ornate, some are very plain, and most of them are very old, weathered, and worn.

I'm in a state of utter amazement but I nonetheless manage to pull Melissa into the parking lot which faces the front of the cemetery and I choose a parking space in front of a historical marker and pull into it. I begin reading the marker, which starts with: "Melrose Cemetery, Formerly known as the 'Banana Burying Grounds,'" and then the sign goes on to explain a brief history of the farming community of... *Banana*, Florida.

My lord.

All I can do is sit here on my idling bike, staring at the marker and re-reading it again and again, occasionally moving my gaze out into the cemetery to look at the old, old tombstones, some of which are small tombstones, and some of which are medium-sized, and some of which are large; some are ornate, some are very plain, and most of them seem to be very old, weathered, and worn. My dream come true.

I am sitting face-to-face with the reality that was conveyed to me in last night's dream, a reality that was totally and completely unbeknownst to me...until now.

I contemplate this powerful new reality in my life: Something, someone, has chosen to convey true and verifiable information to me in a dream, making me aware of a time and a place that I never knew existed, and then they have enabled me to find this place today. Here I sit, staring at its reality. I'm flabbergasted. I've had over 800 paranormal experiences in my life so far, and I've never become jaded...I'm as excited and amazed by the most recent ones as I was when the very first one happened to me. And today I'm certainly excited and amazed. In fact, "excited and amazed" may be an understatement given the circumstances.

I back Melissa up, turn her around, back her into the same parking space, shut her off and dismount. I take a few photos of the historical marker and of Melissa parked in front of it and the cemetery.

And then I walk into the cemetery, still amazed that I am in this place.

In my dream the dates on some of the tombstones dated back into the 1800s, and as I slowly wander through the cemetery and inspect the graves I see that some of the dates on the tombstones read: "Born 1818;" "Died 1871 at 95 years old;" "Born 1868." Some of the inscriptions and dates in some of these old stones are scratched into the tombstones by hand. I'm speechless.

I continue my exploration of...Banana...reading tombstones, taking photos, pausing to talk to some of the cemetery workers who tell me to make sure that I see the Iron Cross awarded to a Civil War veteran of the Confederate Army. I learn that there are veterans of eight wars interred here from as far back as the Mexican-American War and the Civil War. What an incredible burying ground!

And I finally take a deep breath and ask the Other Side, "Okay... why am I here? Why have you shown this to me in a dream and then brought me here today to verify its reality?"

And I receive a tremendously frustrating answer: "We will not tell you just yet. You are on just the first stage of this mystical journey, and you will have to return here more times before everything is fully revealed and finally becomes clear to you." And that's all that they choose to tell me; for now.

*Damn!* In spite of my psychic gift and my long history of interaction with the Other Side I'm human like everyone else: I'm impatient too, and I want all of my answers to be clear and to come to me all at once instead of me having to work for them and ponder things through before an understanding is finally achieved. But one thing that I have learned from my interactions with the Other Side is that they can see a lot farther down the road than I can, and they always have good reasons for making me wait.

So I bridle my impatience and continue to explore the cemetery. It's a peaceful place, but, as all such places are it's full of the pain of loss of life and the loss of loved ones. Most heart-rending to me are the small flat gravestones that are inscribed, "Known Only to God." One tiny gravestone's entire epitaph is the inscription of only a single word: "Unknown." Imagine that: *unknown.*

Imagine having lived an entire life: being born; playing as a child; perhaps learning to ride a horse; learning to swim; growing up; having sex for the first time; falling in love; eating a favorite meal; becoming an adult; perhaps falling in love and starting a family of your own; laughing; sighing; crying; and finally...dying. *And no one even knows that you were here! Unknown!* Dear God. Even now as I write this, years later, my eyes well up with tears.

On one old stone which lists the date of death as being in the 1800s there is a hand-engraved inscription written in cursive. I'm guessing a family member took a nail or something else to use as a scribe and, in the same manner in which we write in wet concrete, wrote the first four lines of a touching poem in the then wet tombstone, which reads:

*A precious one from us has gone*
*The voice we loved is stilled*
*A vacant place is in our home*
*Which never can be filled*

There are benches scattered throughout the cemetery and so I sit down and gaze out over this incredible memorial to our demise, which has become a confirmation of my dream, and also a method of communication from the Other Side. But of what significance, of what meaning? What do they want me to learn from this place?

Has someone who once lived in Banana called to me from the Other Side because they needed me to remember this place as it was, or perhaps to remember *them* so that they are not forgotten? Has one of the shades of those underneath one of the tiny markers engraved "Unknown" risen from the grave to call out to me in my dream? *Come see me. Come visit me. Memorialize me. Please, don't forget me.*

I don't know; I'm not given that information this day. I know that this will be an ongoing investigation for me, and that there will be more discoveries made before I can finally put the pieces of this particular puzzle together in a meaningful way.

But one thing that I know to do before I leave the cemetery and mount up to ride is to say a short prayer for the folks of Banana; especially the ones who were laid to rest as Unknown.

And I make a promise to old Banana that I'll be back, and that I will complete this psychic mission with which I've been entrusted. I'll return until the Other Side makes clear to me the purpose and meaning of my dream and my visits.

And as I mount up and ride away from old Banana I take away the knowledge that the Other Side can communicate with us in dreams that are absolutely specific, logical, meaningful, real, and verifiable.

Have you ever had dreams that came true, dreams that were precognitive or that foretold a situation in your life?

I've known many people who have.

We're all encouraged to pay closer attention to our dreams, and, after having had this experience I can understand why: What other dramatic examples of this type of dream world communication could we receive if we were to ask for this help, this information, this revelation every night before going to sleep, and then making a careful record of the results? Who knows what problems we could solve in our daily lives, what wonderful inventions we might be made aware of, what helpful guidance we might receive that would serve to benefit our daily lives and perhaps the lives of others?

And as for Banana...why in the world, if the Other Side could reveal such explicit and accurate information to me in a dream, why couldn't they also show me who sent that dream to me, and for what purpose? Why do I have to keep going back to Banana to continue to learn the reason or reasons why?

My best guess is that it continues to teach me the life lessons that I need to learn about trust, and perseverance...continuing to strive for spiritual insight and understanding even though it's difficult and does not come to me easily at certain times. Going back to reliance on *that* word again: Faith.

Maybe it's time for you to begin to keep a dream journal of your very own. Who knows what insights you'll receive and where you'll be led? Just remember to be patient, and that the revelations and information that come to you in bits and pieces may be just as important, or ultimately more so, than a dream which contains an entire revelation in one night.

Sweet dreams.

## Epilogue: The Second Trip to Banana

I've parked Melissa in the same parking space as before, and I've begun to wander about the cemetery, which is now beginning to be somewhat of a familiar landscape to me.

"Okay guys," (*Guys*…my collective term of endearment for the retinue of spirits that provide me with guidance from the Other Side) "I'm back. What's today's bit of enlightenment that you have to reveal to me here in old Banana?" Will the next piece of this strange puzzle fall into place for me today? And lo and behold it does!

I notice a couple of gentlemen wandering around the cemetery together; besides myself they're the only other souls here…at least in the flesh, that is.

I feel like I should approach them. I've always been gregarious and I've never been afraid to strike up a conversation with strangers; it's usually lead to pleasant encounters with others and sometimes I've even been able to help them with some problem or issue that they've been facing. So I slowly walk over to where they're also meandering about and I hail them with a friendly greeting.

Now I've learned something about my life as a psychic: people are either fascinated by me; frightened of me; or convinced that I'm an unwitting tool of Satan. So I've developed a fail-safe introduction over the years: after evaluating the person or persons I've just met–psychically as well as by normal means–I will then explain to them

25

that I am a professional psychic and paranormal investigator, or, if I discern that they would be antagonistic toward me if I reveal such information then I explain to them that I am an artist, a painter and a photographer, which is absolutely true.

My hand found a pencil at an early age and I was instantly pleasurably addicted to making art, in a very literal sense of the word. I could no more not make art than I could successfully quit eating or breathing. I studied art independently and at the university level, and I took a course in professional photography, and over the years I've been in many gallery shows and I have paintings and photographs in private collections all across the United States and in a few other countries as well.

But in talking with these gentlemen today I'm given the go-ahead to introduce myself as a professional psychic...even though immediately afterward both of these gentlemen tell me that they're devout Christians! Wow, guys...what have you gotten me into? This is usually a recipe for a heated argument with final denunciations from the Christian side that I am a tool of The Devil and am hell bound unless I repent of this sulfuric gift. (Never mind the fact that I am a legitimately ordained Christian Reverend, was at one time briefly the associate pastor of a small church, and probably know the Bible inside and out better than those with whom I'm discoursing. Yeah, yeah...don't go there: "for even Satan disguises himself as an angel of light." I ain't he, nor one of his minions.)

I explain to the gentlemen that as a psychic I'm frequently given prophetic dreams, but this dream about Banana and my subsequently finding out that it really existed has topped the list.

One man is skeptical, asking me how I reconcile my psychic gift with the Bible's admonitions against it, but the other man cuts him off short: "Well, what is God if he isn't supernatural? God's paranormal, isn't He? Aren't miracles, visions, healings...aren't all of those things supernatural in nature?"

Well, yes, the other man agrees.

So I tell them that I've written a book about my psychic experiences that relate specifically to my motorcycling, which includes the Banana story. Both of them, including the somewhat skeptical gentleman, immediately state that they would *love* to read it! Is it available now, they ask, and if so where can they buy a copy?

I explain that I haven't found an agent or publisher for it yet, but I give them my website and tell them to keep checking, that when I do get my book published I will announce it there along with information as to how it's available for purchase.

We converse a bit more, exchange pleasant goodbyes, and I head to Melissa to mount up and ride back home.

One of my concerns was how my book would be received among those of strict faiths, and today the Other Side has led me here once again to provide this encounter which has alleviated that particular worry.

Thanks, guys; I appreciate it. And I'll be back soon. Maybe the third time really will be a charm, and the ultimate mystery of the Banana Dream will finally be revealed.

CHAPTER **III**

# Round and Round

A CROP CIRCLE is a sizable pattern, usually circular, created by the flattening of a crop such as wheat, barley, rye, maize, or rapeseed. I.e., grasses.

I was reading a book about crop circles written by a noted researcher and an experiment was mentioned that really piqued my curiosity.

A person had decided that if there is any truth to the speculation that there are intelligent forces behind the appearances of crop circles then an individual should somehow be able to communicate with those intelligences.

So this person asked these intelligences to make a particular shape or design in a specific patch of grass that he designated as the one in which he wanted the pattern to appear; and lo and behold... the exact shape or design he had requested appeared in the exact patch of grass that he had designated!

Now that struck me as a pretty cool experiment to try and replicate, so early one morning I sat on my lanai and spoke softly and I made a verbal request to these intelligences, indicating what type of shape I would like to see appear in my lawn, and designating the area of lawn in which I wanted the shape to appear. I also gave them a time frame: I would like the shape to appear in that particular section of my lawn within a week's time, because we had a yard service and it would be a week until they mowed our lawn again...ample time during the summer season for the fast growing grass to be more than tall enough to notice any type of peculiar depression or design in it.

I then spent a few quiet moments in meditation and contemplation, thanked the intelligences for listening to my request, and then I headed to my garage and fired Melissa up...

My intention is to ride for the entire day, visiting two or three of my favorite state parks in the process, and covering hundreds of pleasurable miles.

I am blessed with a sunny day, blue sky without a hint of clouds, and a rare enjoyment: not a trace of wind. I had been rather surprised after we had moved to Florida to learn that the wind blows often here, and occasionally it blows fiercely enough to nearly rip me from my bike, and that's on a pretty, sunny day with no storms in sight.

But today there is not a hint of a breeze, I have ample sunshine, a full tank of gas, and a light heart as I pull out of my garage and head out to my first intended destination: a state park that was once the site of a bustling and prosperous plantation where the owners grew sugar cane, rice, cotton, and indigo, a plant with many desirable properties: it was used for medicinal purposes and also as a dye, among other things.

The plantation was destroyed in the Second Seminole War of 1836, and now the ruins of the former plantation–a sugar mill; a unique spring house; several wells; and the crumbling foundations of the plantation house and slave cabins–have been preserved.

At this state park, as well as others, I have previously taken my digital voice recorder with me and I have been able to record spirit voices, a phenomenon known as EVP, or Electronic Voice Phenomenon. Electronic Voice Phenomena are words and phrases found on electronic recordings but are not the result of intentional recording or rendering. In other words, no voice from anyone visible is speaking, and the person making the recordings seldom hears any of the voices until they analyze the recordings.

Today however I will receive a different type of communication from the realm of spirit, and one that is unique to my experiences with spirit messages.

When I am outdoors in Nature, where I most love to be, I have trained myself to be especially sensitive to manifestations of and communications from the Other Side. This day will not be in short supply of these amazing manifestations and communications.

I arrive at the first park, secure my bike, and begin my first short hike of the day on one of the paths.

As I walk the woods I watch the path right in front of me (always wary of the six deadly species of venomous snakes which are everywhere in Florida), and I scan the areas to my left and right (to make sure that I'm not about to become a tasty meal for a bear or a panther that might be lurking in the brush), and I also scan as far up the path as I can see. And in looking far ahead up the path I'm walking on now I discover the first paranormal manifestation that I will experience today. And what an unusual manifestation it is.

About a hundred feet away, maybe a little farther, is a small clump of Florida's ubiquitous saw palmetto, which is a small palm with spiny leaves. This little clump is a very young growth because the fronds are only about two feet high, but one frond in particular catches my eye immediately, because it's waving at me.

I stop walking and focus my stare on this little frond. Its stem appears to be bending about six or eight inches up from the ground, the bend forming a type of hinge on which the remainder of the frond vigorously but smoothly swings to one side and then back to the other, an arc which is about one to two feet wide. It's a most bizarre and a most unusual behavior, something that's definitely out of the ordinary. The little plant looks like a natural metronome.

I suspect that a gust of wind must be moving through the forest, but my glance all around the woods confirms what I already know: there is not a breeze stirring anywhere. Besides, if the wind were making one frond in the clump wave back and forth so dramatically then the other fronds would also be affected, and they're not. The other fronds of this plant are all perfectly still.

30

I resume walking toward the waving frond, watching it carefully as I get closer. It's not wavering around like it would be if the wind were blowing it; it's just methodically waving back and forth on the exact same arc over and over and over.

And then I get close enough that I hear it, and the sound is audible from a good thirty feet away...the metronomic ticking as the stem is bent sideways each time the frond waves back and forth: *tick-tick-tick-tick-tick*.

I stop in front of the little frond and gaze down at it. *Tick-tick-tick-tick-tick* as it waves its merry little greeting to me.

I glance around me once more; not a leaf is stirring anywhere in the forest.

I bend down on one knee and place my face close to the frond, and I examine it closely from all angles looking for a snake, or a bug, or a super-tiny bird, or a *whatever* that might be causing this extremely odd behavior. Nothing; there is absolutely nothing odd or unusual about this plant, and the stem is normal except for the bend in it whenever the plant arcs one way and then the other. There are no bugs, no insects, and no critters of any kind that are visible, and there is nothing I can see inside the stem of the plant that is chewing or eating or moving about internally. Everything is normal; everything is whole. *Tick-tick-tick-tick-tick*.

I take a count: If this little frond *were* a metronome it would be moving back and forth at about 140 beats per minute. This thing is really rocking.

I stand up and place my hands on my hips and I continue to watch the little plant. I'm gobsmacked. There is no logical, reasonable explanation for why this is happening. The little frond keeps up its steady rhythm. This has been going on for a good 10 minutes now. A thought flashes through my mind: *is saw palmetto a type of grass?* It's probably not, but the thought causes me to reflect back on my earlier request to the intelligences. Could this be a sign from them?

Or could it be nature spirits saying hello to me by waving the frond back and forth? Or could the frond itself be exhibiting intelligence and knowledge of my presence?

After shaking my head in disbelief, I wave back to the little plant, and I talk to it: "Well, hello my little friend. It's nice of you to welcome me to the forest, and to wave hello to me. Thank you." I believe in nature spirits, and in communicating with nature; I know, it sounds a little "New Age-y," but if you'd had the many supernatural experiences that I've had in the woods, you'd talk to the nature spirits too. And yes, they do talk back. I have recorded proof.

I pause and get quiet to see if some other paranormal phenomenon will occur, but nothing does and I don't receive any particular message from the spirits, so I tell the little plant goodbye and I continue walking the path. I look back from time to time and the little frond is still waving. It hasn't stopped or slowed, and again, the air is still and there is no wind.

I reach the end of the hiking path and turn around to retrace my steps back to my parked motorcycle. Sure enough, as I get close enough to see my little plant friend I can see that it's still waving at the same frequency and with the same wide arc as it was before; it hasn't stopped. There is still no wind; *not a leaf is stirring in the forest.*

I stop and stand before the little plant and I reexamine it once again, just to make sure that there is no normal explanation for this incredible behavior. The little plant is normal, except that it continues to wave that one frond back and forth, back and forth, back and forth. *Tick-tick-tick-tick-tick.*

This plant's supernatural behavior has continued to make this motion in this exact same repetition for a good 20-30 minutes now that I'm aware of. With this vigorous motion repeated over and over for such a length of time the "hinge" point of the stem should be showing considerable wear and tear, or should even be beginning to split or to break in two. Incredibly the stem is perfectly intact.

"Well, my little friend," I say, "I've enjoyed this experience. Thank you. I've enjoyed communing with you, and I speak a blessing and peace to you, and I hope you return the same to me. I'm going to be going now as I have a lot of miles I want to put in today and it's a beautiful day to enjoy a nice, long ride. You take care, and I'll see you again soon."

I wait to see if anything else will happen, but nothing does. But it does dawn on me again that this strange happening is occurring on the very morning that I've made my request to the crop circle intelligences, and it's unique to my repertoire of experiences that I've had in nature, paranormal or otherwise. I wonder if this *is* somehow connected to my request. But then again I've experienced *over 800* amazing paranormal experiences in my life, and maybe, for whatever reason, this is just another of the things that I routinely see and experience. Or is it? I shrug, and I decide I'll try to make more sense of it later; right now I've got miles to cover, and more state parks to visit.

I wave a final goodbye to the little plant and head up the trail to the parking area. As I walk I look back from time to time and the little plant is still waving at me, just as vigorously as before. Wow. What an amazing start to my day.

I fire up my big v-twin and roar out of the park on my way to more adventure. What I don't know yet is that at my next stop I will experience not just one, but *two* incredible happenings.

Are the crop circle intelligences responding to me?


Even though it's early morning I've already worked up a sweat, walking the hiking trail in the Florida heat.

I've waved goodbye to the little waving frond, fired up my bike, and now I'm back on the road roaring along at highway speeds, and the wind blast feels good to me and helps to cool me down.

I put the incident with the waving frond behind me for now; I'll think about it more in depth later, when I'm once again sitting on my lanai with a cold beer in my hand, but for now I must focus my attention on my ride: I've been riding motorcycles since I was about fifteen or sixteen years old, and I know all too well the hazards that a motorcyclist faces on the road. If a biker wants to live long he or she must focus all of his faculties on the task at hand: avoiding not only the hazards of the road that might be an inconvenience to or cause minor damage to a car but which could mean certain death to a biker, as well as watching out for and dodging the idiots who drive with a death grip on their steering wheels and a thousand-yard unblinking and unseeing stare, never utilizing their peripheral vision, and seemingly unaware that they're *not* the only person on the road that day.

Yes, it's dangerous, but it's *fun!* I've even gone so far as to state that if you really do long-distance biking right the sensation almost ranks right up there with having good sex. *(Almost...)* So I enjoy my ride in spite of the hazards of the road and the idiots in their cages, and the big v-twin purrs like a kitten, hungrily gobbling up miles of highway and begging for more and before I know it I'm at my next destination, which is another of Florida's beautiful state parks.

At this park I've also captured EVP–the recording of spirit voices–and unlike most EVP, which you have to clean up electronically and listen to over and over again in order to try and make out what the voices are saying, here in this state park I have captured a spirit voice so astonishingly clear and audible that you can hear it directly from my recorder's speaker without even having to use headphones or enhance the audio digitally. It sounds like a young child's voice, and it clearly and distinctly says, "Peek-a-boo." I guess the spirits want me to know that they're watching me as I meander about the woods.

But today I decide that I'm probably not going to try and record any spirit voices; instead I'm going to walk some more for exercise and because I enjoy being outdoors. I have always loved to be outside, in nature, ever since I was a small child. Yeah, I was one of those kids who had to be called repeatedly to come in from outside and I was always begging for "Just another half hour, please!"

But first, before I begin my hike through the woods in this state park, I have an old friend to retrieve. I hide him away in this very same park–very carefully–every time I leave, so he should be tucked away safe and sound in my secret hiding place. First though, a little bit about him; and why I use him.

I've got bad knees; well, that ain't the only thing that's gone south, but that's the primary reason that I have come to rely on my friend.

My friend is a small fallen tree branch which is about two to three inches in diameter and about five to five and a half feet tall; just perfect for use as a sturdy walking stick. I found this branch in a previous visit to the park and some days it is a real help when my knees want to give out but I want to hike the trails.

I came to develop a real affection for this walking stick as a gift from nature and I decided that I wanted to be able to use it anytime that I came to this park, but that I didn't want anyone else to find it, so, every time that I finished my hike I would make sure no one else was around and I would stash my walking stick underneath some underbrush back up under a thicket of trees so that I would be the only person who knew where it was and so that I could easily retrieve it from its hiding place every time that I came to the park.

Subsequently I learned, online, about a collapsible aluminum walking stick and I ordered one. It was sturdy, folded down small enough to fit into one of my saddlebags, had a compass in the tip of the nicely padded handle, and it was convenient to use in the outdoors; actually it was a delight to use, so I had decided that I would leave my old wooden walking stick propped against a tree along the trail hoping that some other hiker might find it and use it and maybe enjoy it as much as I had.

I dug my old friend out from his hiding place, pronounced a blessing on him, and left him leaning against a tree next to the hiking trail. The tree was sitting on the left hand side of the hiking trail (walking the trail "forward"), the tree's base sat very close to the trail itself, and I propped the stick against it at roughly a sixty degree angle, not against either side of the tree but with the tip of the stick close to the trail and the head of the stick leaning against the tree trunk. As you hiked the trail and saw the tree and the stick it would look as if a branch were growing from the trunk of the tree toward the trail and terminating itself at the ground. This description is important, so please remember it.

And so as time came to pass sure enough, the next time I walked this particular trail the walking stick was gone. Weeks went by and I never saw it anywhere along the hiking trails, or anywhere else in the park. Even though I was enjoying my new high-tech walking stick I kind of missed my old friend a little bit and I hoped that whoever had taken him was treasuring his aid and assistance in the great outdoors as I once had.

And then one day as I neared the end of the hiking trail (once again walking the trail "forward") there was a branch propped against a tree which stood next to the hiking trail. This tree was also sitting on the left hand side of the hiking trail, the tree's base sat very close to the trail itself, and the stick was propped against it at roughly a sixty degree angle, not against either side of the tree but with the tip of the stick close to the trail and the head of the stick leaning against the tree trunk. Exactly as I had left it but in a previous location along the trail.

I'm thinking to myself that it *couldn't* be, especially after all of this time, but yes, as I inspected the branch it was indeed my old friend.

Now this branch had some oddities about it that made it easy for me to differentiate it from, say, ten other similar branches you might have mixed it in with. It's unique, and readily identifiable. There was absolutely no question that this was my old friend come back to me. I felt warm-hearted, and I talked to my old walking stick at length. It was like reuniting with an old friend that you haven't seen in awhile.

So I had taken my old friend and had put him back into hiding, concealing him in the underbrush back up under some trees as I had done before. After that incident I had found another unique branch that I sometimes used as a walking stick and I had also hidden it with the first one.

Sometimes I would use my aluminum walking stick, and sometimes I would go and dig out my old friend (or occasionally, my new one) to accompany me on the trail.

So today I decide that I'll go and get my old friend to accompany me in my walk. I want the feeling of this unique branch in my hand as I hike the trails...the feeling of nature's wood in my hands seems to connect me even more with the enjoyment of the outdoors.

So I go to my secret hiding place and I lift up the underbrush and my old friend is not there. The other branch that I stashed with him is there, but my first original branch has vanished. Now remember, this is all occurring after I had asked the crop circle intelligences for a sign. And what is a large portion of this underbrush that has concealed my friend for so long? *Grass.*

I use the newer branch I had found to dig around in the underbrush to see if it might simply have overgrown my original branch, but no matter how much I look I have to acknowledge the fact that the branch has literally simply vanished. My old friend is gone, never to be seen again. I feel a little sad, as well as somewhat bemused.

So here was the first of today's unusual experiences at *this* park: my reappearing walking stick has now vanished; I shake my head and grab the remaining branch to use as a walking stick on my hike.

After I walk for maybe half an hour I round a curve in the trail and there is a single leaf suspended vertically in the middle of the trail about eight to twelve inches off the forest floor; just one leaf, slowly rotating. And the wind is still calm.

I walk around the leaf until I catch the light just right, and I can see that the leaf is suspended by a long, *long* single strand of spider silk which is attached only to the leaf's very tip end and the long strand of silk stretches up high into a tree. It's like this leaf was attached by its stem end to a long rope of spider silk and then it bungee jumped, stopping just short of the forest floor. *How bizarre.*

I guess the leaf's rotation could be ascribed to the strand of silk untwisting under the strain of the leaf's weight, but it certainly couldn't be ascribed to the wind, for there is not the slightest breeze at the moment. The leaf isn't swaying, but is simply slowly rotating.

Wow. My walking stick has disappeared from its secure hiding place, and this lone leaf is suspended by an unbelievably long strand of spider silk directly in the middle of my pathway.

Okay, that's a total of *three* incredible experiences so far today, and it's not even close to noon yet. I take my pocket camera out and take a picture of the suspended leaf.

I finish my hike, hide my one remaining branch, and head back to the parking area and my beloved bike.

I'm used to experiencing a plethora of paranormal events, but the relatively rapid-fire occurrences this morning in seeming response to my request is really giving me some serious food for thought. I'm convinced now that something very unusual and very special is happening. I'm honored to be privy to these supernatural demonstrations.

These three events are mind-blowing enough all by themselves, but little do I know that *four more* astonishing experiences await me: one I will experience while I'm en route to the next state park I want to visit; another will occur at that park; and two more experiences await me when I arrive home. I'm gonna need that beer after all.


So I'm flying down the highway on my bike en route to the third state park I want to visit today, enjoying the scenery, when I notice a disturbance in the tall grass off on the right shoulder up ahead.

It looks to me like it's a dust devil, the small whirlwind that can wreak temporary havoc with a motorcycle if the wind is strong enough, but the dust devil isn't making progress toward the road, but seems to be stationary instead. A thought immediately crosses my mind: *this is the only wind I've seen today.*

As I get closer I can see that the dust devil is whirling the tall grass flat, into the shape of...*a crop circle!* The wind is flattening the grass into a perfect circle about fifteen to twenty feet in diameter.

*Is this my sign?*

I decide that as interesting as this is it's not my specifically requested sign, because it's not in my yard where I requested the formation to appear. *Still...*

Okay, I may have to give the crop circle intelligences this one, even though it's *not* in my yard. I've learned over the years that we can request a specific sign and sometimes that sign may appear at a time and in a place not of our choosing but yet it will still be an appropriate answer or response to our request.

What an amazing thing I've just witnessed.

As exciting as this phenomenon is I'm flying along at highway speed and I can't allow myself to lapse into a reverie; I'll think about it later, when I relax on my lanai at day's end. I give a little salute to the crop circle and as an acknowledgement of thanks to the Powers That Be, and then I turn the wick up on the bike and enjoy the feeling of speed experienced on two wheels.

Before long I'm at the third state park I've visited today. This park is a gigantic deep "bowl" in the ground, the top circumference of which is encircled by a paved roadway about two miles long.

Sometimes I park in the lot and walk the paved road and also walk some of the hiking trails. Sometimes I ride Melissa around the paved road, which descends down into the bottom of the "bowl," and park in a lower parking area and sit overlooking the ponds or hike to one of the two footbridges in the park.

I've enjoyed a brief hike through this park today and nothing else unusual has occurred, so I decide I'll leave this, the third state park I've visited today, and finish my day up with some aimless riding on the highways and bi-ways of Florida. More time on the bike equals more fun.

I'm riding Melissa very slowly on the paved road and I'm getting close to exiting the park. On the right-hand side of the road is a large stand of bamboo. As I get closer to it one of the tall stalks of bamboo very slowly begins to bow over. I can't believe my eyes. It's as if a giant who is 20 feet tall or more is bending over and grabbing the top of this stalk of bamboo and very slowly and gently bending it over toward the ground to form an arch across the roadway.

I ride as slowly as I can, keeping the big bike balanced at the pace of about a slow walk, watching this spectacle unfold. The stalk of bamboo continues to bend over in a graceful curve until its tip is almost touching the roadway on the other side, in effect making an arch that I have to ride through, the apex of which is so low that I have to duck down on my bike to make it under and through.

After I ride under the gracefully arched stalk of bamboo I stop and dismount to inspect it. There is absolutely nothing I can find that accounts for this behavior. I've been an outdoorsman all of my life, and I've never seen anything like this before. In my mind I flash back to the incredibly bizarre behavior of the palm frond, and now here is this tall stalk of bamboo gently bent over the roadway by unseen forces. There is no break in the stalk of bamboo; it's just gently bent over the roadway in a graceful arch, and once again a close and careful examination reveals no normal reason for this behavior.

And then it dawns on me: bamboo is…*grass*. The crop circles are always associated with some type of grass. Wheat, in which many crop circles appear, is a type of grass. Lawns are varieties of grasses. And bamboo is classified as a type of grass.

I'm blown away. I've experienced some definite supernatural signs today; I've experienced some occurrences for which there can only be paranormal explanations, and some of these experiences have had specific and undeniable connections to grass, including the crop circle formed on the shoulder of the highway, and the bamboo.

I shake my head in amazement, verbally speak words of acknowledgement and thanks to the Powers That Be, and remount Melissa to ride out of the park.

As I ride away I stop and look back, and the bamboo stalk is still arched over the roadway. Amazing; absolutely amazing.

I say a silent word of thanks for all I've experienced this day, and then I leave the park to enjoy my bike, just to ride with no particular destination in mind.

I enjoy several more miles on the bike, and when I get home I've covered between 200-300 miles today. For me it's been an average day's ride mileage-wise, but anything but average otherwise.

I park Melissa in the garage and take a moment to listen to her ticks and pings, the sounds emanating from her hot engine as the metal cools down. To me it's like a little song she sings to me. I smile, and lovingly pat her gas tank.

And then it's finally time to enjoy sitting on my lanai with a cold beer at day's end.

And just when I think that I can finally sit and ruminate about today's events I'm confronted with yet *another* odd experience: when I left this morning the chair in which I had been sitting was right by the back door; now it's all the way over to the edge of the lanai. Nothing else on the lanai has been moved, only the chair that I was sitting in when I addressed the intelligences.

I ask my wife if she has moved that chair for any reason whatsoever, but no, she hasn't even been on the lanai today. We've had no service people come to our house today. I know our neighbors and none of them would trespass on our property, certainly not to move one chair while leaving everything else on my lanai intact.

I glance quickly at the grass in my yard, but there's nothing there; no crop circle has been formed in my yard. Still and all I've experienced the waving frond; my disappearing walking stick; the leaf suspended in the middle of the hiking trail; the dust devil forming a crop circle in the grass by the highway; the bamboo arching over the roadway; and now my chair having been moved across the lanai. Six distinct experiences after I made my request early this morning for a sign from the intelligences behind the crop circle phenomenon, and two of those experiences had to do with grass, the typical medium in which crop circles appear.

I have experienced an intelligent communication this day; as a matter of fact, I've experienced several intelligent communications. There's more than meets the eye here, there's more for me to learn, more knowledge for me to try and apply to this investigation: could EVP be intensified in crop circles? Are there apparitions that appear in or around crop circles? And what about the supposed connections between UFOs and crop circles?

My mind is in a whirl.

It grows dark, and my wife joins me on the lanai and we listen to some music and discuss the day's events. We both agree that it's pretty astonishing to have experienced all of these occurrences after having made the request that morning.

The mosquitoes worsen and my wife heads inside; I spray mosquito repellant on myself, grab another cold beer, and stay outside on the lanai to enjoy not only the music but the bright stars glistening overhead and the sounds of the night.

And then it happens: and to me it's the most bizarre experience that I've had this day.

This one particular star suddenly grows brighter as I gaze at it, and then it seems to rapidly move closer toward me in the sky. And then, it splits in two. I shake my head to clear my vision, but no, the twin star is still there. I quickly glance around the lanai, looking at the other pieces of furniture which are softly lit by the kitchen light coming through the windows and glass doors; I look at the blazing Tiki torches, and my radio sitting on the table which is close by. I'm not seeing double; everything else is sharp and in clear focus.

I look back up at the double star, and I can't keep the thought out of my head: something, someone, *is looking at me*. The bright twin stars are spaced just far enough apart to look like blazing eyes gazing down upon me. Suddenly the doubled star rejoins into one and just as quickly seems to recede back into the night sky.

The thought that something or someone has such incredible power as to be able to cause such amazing manifestations not only on the Earth but in the heavens as well is mind-boggling! In spite of all of the paranormal events I have encountered in my life the seven I have experienced today rank up there at the top of the list.

I sit outside for a long time, enjoying the music and the night and the stars and my cold beer, pondering all of these incredible things that I have been privileged to witness today.

Shortly thereafter, I go inside for the night.

It's obvious by both the quantity and quality of today's experiences that some intelligence or group of intelligences has heard me and responded to me. And not just once, but several times.

The sheer quantity of today's experiences are overwhelming, accompanied by the fact that all of them were powerful physical manipulations of physical matter: Spirit has demonstrated that it is capable of moving objects, communicating via objects, revealing things, hiding things, producing signs, and making the very stars in the heavens dance around the night sky!

But to what purpose? To what intent?

Primarily, I think, to let us know that our requests are heard; that the Other Side does hear and many times act upon our requests. They certainly did for mine!

I think also that we can learn from these experiences that sometimes we get a plethora of answers or manifestations in response to our requests, and other times only one or maybe even none.

*Why?*

I've asked that question more times than I can count.

There are certain theories, some of which make some sense if considered. For example, one theory is that communication between the physical and spiritual realms may be likened to communicating from one continent to another via shortwave radio: some days or nights the conditions are perfect and communication is as clear as a bell and lasts for some time; other days or nights the conditions aren't quite so perfect and communication is spotty, or short-lived; and still other days or nights conditions are difficult and communication is impossible. From my personal experience this seems to make sense; it's a good metaphor for communication with the Other Side.

There's a whole rich history of occultists, metaphysicians, shamans, witch doctors, medicine men, mediums, psychics, and even theologians trying to conjure just the right environment in order to successfully communicate with the unseen realms. I myself have never encountered a time, in all of my years of reading for clients, that I could not read for a client. But I have become aware over the years of periods of time when that feeling of connection to the Other Side was not quite as strong as it was during others.

I have been blessed with a tremendous amount of meaningful, even lifesaving spiritual experiences, and yet there have been times that I have found Heaven to be as brass, and my prayers and attempts at communication and efforts to produce positive energies toward some worthwhile goal were frustrated and seemed to bear no useful fruit at all.

Which has led me, and certain others, to believe that the Other Side is capable of seeing a lot farther down the road then we can, and they know when the timing is, or isn't, right for the achievement or fulfillment of some desired course of action. Again, we go back to lessons of trust and faith.

And then I think that sometimes we are made to learn to persevere. Truly good things don't come easily to anyone: the champion athlete, although blessed and gifted with the proper genetics from birth and inherently possessing enormous physical talent for a certain category of sport, nevertheless must train diligently if he or she is ever to rise to the pinnacle of their chosen athletic contest.

Without copping out I also seriously do believe that another type of answer we may receive is that we need to wait awhile for conditions to improve, i.e. "Not right now. But maybe later."

And then I've learned, both through personal experience and interaction with the lives of others, especially my clients, that sometimes...sometimes the answer is "No."

And that's the hardest one for us to accept and to move on from, but it is essential to be able to take no for an answer and to look ahead if we want to progress in life and not grow stagnant or bitter. To be mature; to act like adults. To show our faith and trust in this higher power that we've entreated.

In the meantime, I encourage you to conduct your own experiments. Who knows what dramatic signs or communications that you might receive?

Just be prepared to accept it if the answer does come, and it is "no."

But if you do begin to receive these dramatic manifestations or communications, show gratitude, say *thank you,* and continue to endeavor to communicate with these powerful beings and energies that, who knows, someday just may save your life, as they have done for me on many an occasion.

# The Ghosts of Olustee

I'M RIDING MELISSA, my beloved motorcycle, and we're cruising up I-95 north into Jacksonville, Florida where I'll pick up I-10 west and ride to the Olustee Battlefield, site of one of the major battles of the Civil War.

I've always wanted to visit a Civil War battlefield in order to perform a paranormal investigation, and to see if any of the ghosts from this war will communicate with me at that particular site.

As I ride I do some thinking on the way; this is my first visit to such a place and I wonder what my psychic senses will tell me about it when I get there. Thinking about the Civil War also gets me to thinking about warfare in general, which is a part of man's inhumanity to man.

I dodge the cager[1] who wants to make me and my motorcycle into a hood ornament and I recall the words from famed nuclear physicist, UFO researcher, and lecturer Stanton Friedman. This is his comment about our so-called civilization: "…a primitive society whose major activity (judging by how its wealth is spent) would certainly appear to be tribal warfare and for whom every new frontier is a new place to do battle."[2]

Lord a'mighty, we do love to fight, don't we? By "we" I mean "all of us" here on this old planet named Earth. And here am I, en route to a memorial to war in all of its hideous glory.

I don't know why we worship war; it mystifies me that we do. The Bible, our Christian Holy Book, is not only full of war, it glorifies it! God, "our" God, even commanded his followers to commit genocide, which is the systematic killing of all of the people from a different national, ethnic, or religious group. God's instructions about such murders were explicit, and abundant; the following Biblical quotes are only two of a *plethora* of Biblical examples where God demands mass slaughter: "In the cities of the nations the Lord is giving you as an inheritance, do not leave alive anything that breathes." (Deuteronomy 20:16) "And they utterly destroyed all that was in the city, both man and woman, young and old, and ox, and sheep, and ass, with the edge of the sword." (Joshua 6:21) And there are many other, even more horrifying passages to read, our "loving" god instructing his followers to run pregnant women through the belly with the sword; and he was so despising of one peoples that he instructed that there not even be left alive anything that pisses against the wall…in other words, kill the dogs, too.

Most religions have a veneer of peace and goodwill toward man, but if you scratch below the surface the hostility and condemnation toward others who do not subscribe to the same belief system soon becomes evident, and many times expresses itself in violence: the shooting of the abortion clinic doctor; the murder of a young gay man; Manifest Destiny; 9-11; ISIS.

And we all engage in war. Hell, if we can't find *the Other* with whom to fight, we will fight amongst ourselves: American Indian tribes fought with and killed each other; black-skinned people kill other black-skinned people (Google "necklacing" for one horrific modern-day example); white-skinned people kill other white-skinned people; the Baptist church up the street can't see eye to eye with the doctrine espoused by the Baptist church down the street. Preacher opposes preacher, family members are at odds with one another, races are at odds with one another, and country opposes country: as I predicted many years ago we have returned to Cold War status, as Russia strived to become a Superpower and has achieved that infamous and dangerous stature yet once again.

And some of us glorify war: "Battle is the most magnificent competition in which a human being can indulge. It brings out all that is best..." – General George S. Patton.

As a whole we are indeed a pugnacious lot, aren't we? As I frequently say to my wife: "There's something wrong with us critters here on this old planet."

It's early morning as I complete my ride and pull into the Olustee Battlefield State Park parking lot, and I'm the only person here. I dismount and secure my bike, and I'm immediately struck by how peaceful the atmosphere is; I would expect to be psychically assaulted by sensations of loss, sorrow, violence, remorse, and grief, but instead I'm lulled into a sense of calm. It's an odd feeling to have in such a place, and it's highly unexpected.

But I've noticed the sensation of that unexpected calm when exploring other areas that were once visited with extreme violence. It's almost as though Mother Earth herself tries to put a psychic bandage on the wound in hopes that it will eventually heal.

After lingering beside my bike for a moment I decide I'll start today's adventure by exploring the visitor center. I walk into the small building which contains a seating area in front of a TV, on which is playing, on an endless loop, a documentary about Olustee and the Civil War.

I can maintain an incredibly long attention span if I choose to, but I'm pretty selective about my documentaries–I'm pretty selective about most TV shows and movies, actually–but I sit down to watch this one and it takes me about two minutes to become bored to tears, so I exit onto the grounds to explore. I'd rather watch the psychic movie unfold in my head as I tune into the vibrations from this hallowed killing field.

I wander around looking at the cannons, the monuments, and the land. I'm particularly struck by one large monument which reminds me of an overgrown Rook from a monstrously large Chess set. I take several photos and I hope that I'll see ghosts in one or two of them;

I'm disappointed later when I have the film developed and there are no ghosts to be seen.

But the ghosts are here. I feel them. I sense them. And even though the battle waged fierce over all of this countryside I feel an urge to move away from this touristy area into the forest proper. Here in the touristy area man will tell me his truth the best he can. In the forest where I can focus on making contact with the Other Side, I will receive higher truth, without any distractions to either my physical or psychic senses.

But I've only gone a short distance toward the forest when I think that my choice of days to have made this trip may have been a mistake because damn it to hell, they're having a friggin' Civil War reenactment! I hate reenactments. I hate them. I don't do reenactments. I don't do renaissance fairs. I don't do Civil War reenactments. I don't do old west reenactments. I hate reenactments of any kind, because they're just people playing dress up and pretending to be someone they're not, and probably getting most of it entirely wrong. It reminds me of when we were kids and pretended to be astronauts, pirates, cowboys...anyway, just one man's cynical opinion. If you like 'em, good on ya!

But back to my current dilemma: there's no way that I'll be able to conduct a decent paranormal investigation with these people making this hellacious racket. There's a loud volley of musket fire...and then another...and then more...son of a bitch! Now comes the explosive noise of cannons firing, and I can hear what sounds like drumming and the noises of horses' feet pounding the ground, and their whinnies. Good grief!

I guess I should have checked the park's event schedule before I wasted all of my time riding here today hoping for a powerful paranormal experience.

I didn't see the reenactors when I pulled into the parking lot. Maybe they assembled while I was wandering around the visitor center. I begin walking toward a large open field on the property from which the sounds are coming. It's a very short distance that I have to go before I'll have a clear view of the goings-on, and the reenactors sound so close that I hope I don't bumble into some of them. What an embarrassment for us both.

And for the life of me I don't know why I'm going to take a look at this spectacle, other than out of a fleeting curiosity...did I mention that I don't like reenactments of any kind? But that's okay, because when I get a clear view of the whole area I realize I'm being treated to a reenactment alright; but one of the most authentic reenactments of such an event that a person can *ever* experience short of actually having been there at the time, because there's not a soul in the flesh anywhere on this property but me.

I stand transfixed at the sounds of authentic Civil War battle assaulting my ears: more volleys from muskets, their sharp reports piercing the still morning air. Boom! Again there's the thunder of cannon fire. Is that a fife I hear being played with that distant drumming? There! A horse has just emitted a fierce neigh as it plunges into the heat of battle.

The gunfire and the other noises of battle begin to subside and then they fade out entirely, leaving me standing alone in the morning sunshine with nothing but a preternatural quiet to keep me company now.

I stand motionless, staring in the direction from which the sounds of this fierce battle emanated. If you'll pardon the expression, I am quite shell-shocked.


I've closed my gaping mouth and managed to collect my wits somewhat and I thank the Other Side for this powerful demonstration they've provided for me this morning. What an incredibly awesome paranormal drama I've been privileged to hear. This alone has been worth my ride.

I'm so overcome by this experience that it takes me a good little bit to let it all sink in, and when it finally does I decide to return to my idea to explore the forest. I begin to walk the nature trail, my psychic senses alert for any further manifestations.

Erected at intervals alongside the trail are large signs that provide a running commentary on the battle of Olustee. I'm astonished at the savagery that I read about. Just think: on *this very spot* where I'm standing a husband, a father, a son, a friend…died; and for what? For the result that we live in a nation where the "North" and the "South" still curse each other and blacks and whites still nurture prejudices toward one another and none of the other supposed issues over which the Civil War was fought have been resolved: Texas still wants to secede; my god. What useless bloodshed.

I force those thoughts out of my head and I attune to the battle itself, and I'm once again confronted by the unexpected, for here, on this battlefield, as the battle raged long and men lost lives there was an unnatural calm that prevailed inside the men that fought. It's revealed to me that there were few, if any, that acted cowardly, and few, if any, that gave way to feelings of fear. Most, if not all, of the men and most of the animals were possessed of a single-minded focus, and that was to eliminate, as swiftly and as powerfully and as efficiently and as heroically as possible, the enemy: their fellow man.

Indeed there was almost calmness to their resolve, and, among several of the soldiers there was an attitude that this grisly business was akin to fun; some folks honestly enjoy fighting and warfare (and if you doubt that statement of fact, just read Bury My Heart at Wounded Knee). I can feel and relive several of the soldiers' emotions and there was definitely a *mass mindset* of heroic accomplishment prevalent here that served to lift this life and death struggle up onto the plateau of grandiosity, that mass mindset forgetting that each man who was slain was a brother in reality, a brother defined as a fellow human being, and was also *literally* and by blood someone's brother; or father; or son. Not to mention someone's cherished friend; or beloved husband.

Before men took up arms and the cry of battle was given and war was waged with a gruesome ferocity did anyone bother to count the cost of that Minnie ball that was fired into a fellow human being in terms of the loss that would radiate outward from that soldier's death like rings in a pond in ever widening circles that would touch several lives and culminate in that dreaded empty chair around the family dinner table?

No; sadly, the "glories" of war triumphed over human reason that day, and carnage was viewed as not only inevitable, but desirable.

I bow my head for a moment; not to pray, but because I'm humbled and overwhelmed by the revelations that have come upon me. I feel pangs of sorrow because of our collective lust for war. I feel anguish over the fact that people killed other people on a field of battle when, under different circumstances, those selfsame enemies might have loved each other and become the best of friends. I think of the sense of grief, loss, and heartache that the family members who lost loved ones felt, and the mounting frustration they must have felt when they saw that the loss of their loved ones failed to produce any positive change or positive direction for their country after all: from all historical accounts it was politics as usual.

And then one of the larger questions of life that we all face confronts me anew on this battlefield: What has happened to all of the souls of those who were killed here that day?

Have they found peace in the afterlife? Have they expressed remorse for their actions? Do they feel guilt; shame? Or are they ready once again to mount horses made of spirit, instead of flesh and bone, and to continue the mindless, senseless fight on the Other Side? If I was your enemy here, will you still count me as your enemy over there? What a mind-boggling question!

I don't know the answer; and today...I'd rather not know. My psychic senses and my own emotional senses are overwhelmed, and I don't want to absorb any more of this incredible information from the Other Side.

Today, I'd rather know how to cause peace, instead of war, and as I walk, I think.

I wonder why it's so easy to tear things down and yet it's so hard to build things up: did you ever grow a flower or vegetable garden? The very things that we need in order to survive–beauty in the form of flowers, which also provides a means of pollination, leading to more food production; food in the form of fruits and vegetables–are under constant assault from weeds which strive to take over the garden and rob the other plants of crucial nourishment, and from bugs and insects that try their best to devour our flowers and plants until they wither and die. Our very survival is constantly under assault.

It's *hard* to produce something worthwhile in life; it was difficult for me to write this book. It took lots of time, effort, and energy of all kinds, and many revisions. But yet it's easy to disparage, to kill, to demean, to slander, to dump garbage and litter, or to graffiti someone else's pristine wall. Or to start war. You'd think that it would be the other way around, wouldn't you, and yet peace is so hard to work for, so hard to obtain.

Maybe that's why we feel the need to cast our lot with a gang–whether that gang's alliance is with turf, religion, politics, economics, or race–when instead we could be searching for our commonality, for our shared humanness, for ways to benefit all of us instead of just some of us. Maybe it's easier to survive in a group with large numbers that focuses on the status quo instead of truly meaningful change for all. After all, look at what happens to our peacemakers, to those who call for change, for peace, for united humanity…what happened to Kennedy, to King, to Gandhi? We usually kill our peacemakers, but laud our warriors.

I recall those famous words, "I have a dream..." So many of us have had a dream. And it seems that our dreams for human kindness; for shared, uplifting causes; for the true pursuit of happiness for all; it seems that all of those dreams are always being chewed away at by the insects and bugs of disease, prejudice, war, greed, and patrimony–we seem to perpetuate an inheritance of hurtful traditions instead of leaving legacies that will provoke changes that alleviate, instead of contribute to, mankind's sufferings.

We take such pride in our violence, don't we, in spite of its inability to provide meaningful and positive change. Does War add value to any of our lives? I think that the answer to that question is painfully obvious.

Think for a moment: what if we devoted as many resources to producing enough food for every man, woman, and child on this planet as we do to making bombs and tanks and fighter jets?

What if we devoted all of our emotional and intellectual lives to finding our commonalities and what if we engaged in acts of true caring and concern toward every living being on this planet?

I realize with a pang in my heart that wiser men than I have wrestled with these very same questions since time began, and unfortunately we don't seem to be any closer to lasting answers; we only seem to produce more memorials to our anger, our rage, our prejudice, and our pride.

I finish my hike and fire up my bike; I open Melissa's throttle wide, and I urge the iron horses beneath me to flee this blood stained land.

I want to beat my sword into a plowshare, and learn war no more.[3]

1   Cager: Biker terminology for a person whose primary form of transportation is an automobile, or "cage."
2   UFOs: Challenge to SETI Specialists by Stanton T. Friedman (1934-2019 R.I.P.)
3   Isaiah 2:4

# CHAPTER V

# I Didn't Believe in UFOs

## Prologue

AS I WRITE these words I have just celebrated my 62nd birthday. Good lord. There's a popular saying now that, "Old age is not for sissies," and that's damn sure the truth! Sickness, illness, aches, pains, and the looming awareness that our road is growing shorter and shorter in bricks and will eventually run out of bricks! And then we, too, will know exactly what the Other Side is like…firsthand.

It doesn't matter what your rational belief system is, nobody's in a hurry to find out about the Other Side from an in person perspective. Like an old preacher I used to know who said, quoting someone else, "Everybody wants to go to Heaven, but nobody wants to die to get there!"

I sure have seen a lot of life, and most of it has been pretty damn fascinating and interesting, and I've had some really fun and enjoyable times, as well as suffering the typical heartaches that beset us all. But oh my god, the saying is so, so true: "Youth is wasted on the young." Truly, truly, if I only knew *then* what I know *now*. Oh my… to be this young again, with the hopes and beliefs and optimisms of youth and decades of life still left in front of me. And a few less aches and pains to endure…

I'm in my early twenties and I'm in between bikes. I'm temporarily a cager again, and my cage of choice is a hulking nine passenger Oldsmobile Vista Cruiser station wagon. I *love* this monstrous, gas-guzzling beast! It's got a pretty decent AM/FM radio, an ashtray that swivels out of the dashboard (I smoke like the proverbial chimney, and enjoy it, too...pipes, cigarettes, cigars...[I still would but my cardiopulmonary system won't allow it anymore, so I resign myself to the pleasurable memories]), and most importantly this behemoth has these cool windows that run along the roof through which you can see the sky. Because of this feature I've adopted, as my CB handle, the "West Texas Sky Viewer." *This is the one West Texas Sky Viewer. Ya got a copy? Come on back.*

And as young as I am I've already had an *incredible* number of paranormal experiences; but oddly enough, I do not believe in UFOs. I've read the literature; I've talked to some people who have failed to convince me that they've actually seen one; and I've even thrown my psychic radar out there in search of a UFO blip, but so far nothing has convinced me that these objects exist except as delusions or hallucinations.

And I'm sure of my opinion; religiously sure. But I am about to have to switch denominations.

It's about four in the afternoon and as I exit the building the first thing that strikes me, literally, is a strong wind to my face. Living in West Texas, in San Angelo, I'm used to the plentiful and sometimes fierce thunderstorms that pound us, and I'm also used to the occasional tornadoes that we hope to survive without incident, but the energy of *this* storm feels *peculiar*. I sense something unknown and unfamiliar to me weather-wise, and it's got me just a little unsettled.

As I mentioned I'm between bikes. Today I'm driving about in my Vista Cruiser, and to get to my beloved station wagon I merely have to walk a very short distance down the alleyway that runs behind the building I've just exited and then I must cross a narrow two lane street and enter a small parking lot; I can see my car from where I'm standing.

But instead of heading for my car I stay rooted to the spot on which I'm standing, which is right by the building's exterior door that I've just come out of, because there is an impediment to me retrieving my car. A rather large, looming, and intimidating impediment. There is a cloud near my vehicle. No, not a cloud *up there* in the sky, but a cloud which is actually *down in* the parking lot, resting *on* the asphalt.

It is a black, threatening cloud which, it appears, has lowered itself down from the low, dark clouds which cover the sky, and to which it is still attached. The cloud is gently and slowly undulating and churning and folding over on itself, but–seemingly mimicking me–it stays rooted to its spot, too...which is right near my car.

In a very strange twist there is no wind which seems to accompany the appearance of this bizarre cloud, other than the wind which is blowing because of the storm. I would expect, if this were to be a funnel cloud or a small tornado or even a large dust devil, that its rotating and whirling motion would surely be accompanied by a wind significant enough to kick up debris and blow it around the parking lot, but it's not doing so; the cloud seems to exist in a vacuum, in an atmosphere of its own. The bits of dust and debris and litter in the parking lot close to the cloud remain undisturbed.

As I stare at the cloud I notice other ways in which it is not behaving like any other cloud I've ever seen in all of my years of watching the sky and watching the weather here in West Texas: it emits from within itself strange, glowing, fluorescent colors. A large globule of yellow emerges, and then recedes; large globules of brightly glowing greens, blues, violets and oranges emerge here and there from within the cloud, and then recede back into it. I'm both spellbound and mystified, and a little unsettled: I can't decide if this is a funnel cloud turning into a tornado–although if it is it's certainly unlike anything I've ever seen before–and I also can't decide if I should continue to stand here and watch this bizarre scenario continue to unfold or if I should turn around and walk back through the door into the relative safety of the building.

Suddenly, out of the blue, some odd and nonsensical urge arises from within me and I feel as though I'm supposed to walk toward the ominous, weird cloud–like *that's* a rational move–but I decide to obey the bizarre impulse and I take a few halting steps in its direction and *good god almighty* when I do the cloud advances toward me! I stop, and it does too. I take a few steps back and the cloud retreats a small ways. I'm thinking that perhaps I'm going insane–this can't be real. Again I move several steps in its direction, and it moves several feet toward me. I take several steps back and the cloud moves back several feet away from me, almost as if it is playing some type of game with me.

About this time I'm nearly flattened as a friend of mine exits the building and whacks me with the door that I've been standing close to in case I needed to beat a hasty retreat back into the building. He apologizes and asks what in the world I'm doing standing there so close to the door like that and then he says, "Oh wow. It looks like we're in for a storm." And then he spies the cloud down in the parking lot across the street and he says, "What in the hell is that?"

I tell my friend to watch, and I take several steps toward the cloud and it moves several feet toward me, and then I take several steps back and the cloud retreats several feet. I do this a few times, which confirms to me that I am *not* going nuts because my friend sees this phenomenon occur too, and I ask him rather unnecessarily, "Isn't that the weirdest thing you ever saw?" He looks at me like *I'm* the weirdest thing he ever saw and he shakes his head and says a quick "Bye!" and beats it out of there like the Hounds of Hell are after him. *His* car is parked in the opposite direction of the abnormal cloud, and so I'm once again alone with this strange manifestation.

Just as my mounting frustration at my inability to make a decision as to what I should do has grown to epic proportion the cloud suddenly lifts itself back up into the clouds above and all of the clouds begin to move to the south; swiftly.

I decide that it's now or never and while keeping a wary eye on the skies I run to my car. Once safely inside I say aloud, "Damn! What in the hell *was that?!*"

I light a cigarette to calm my nerves; start my car; push the button for my favorite radio station; and pull out of the parking lot.

As I'm driving it begins to rain, and in West Texas it can *really* rain: four to six inches or more in an hour is not uncommon, and in fifteen or twenty minutes time a torrential downpour can cause lawns and streets to flood but the rain I'm experiencing now is unlike anything I've ever seen before. The rain is so dense that it's literally blinding, so blinding that I can barely see to drive, and the dark clouds have only served to reduce visibility further. I turn on my headlights so that other cars can see me better, which proves to be an exercise in futility, because I've driven just a few blocks and the rain is now coming down so heavily that I can no longer look across the front seat and see out my passenger window; I know that there are cars that are angle parked in the parking spaces on the side of the street, and their rear ends are only a few feet away from my car, but I can't see them. My windshield wipers are on high, frantically swatting at the downpour of rain; it doesn't do any good: visibility continues to worsen and the rain falls in such torrents that the wipers can't even pretend to clear the nonstop waterfall running down my windshield. It's only when I am mere inches from the bumper of the car in front of me that my headlights pick it up; I realize that if I try to keep driving in this weather that I'm going to hit someone or someone is going to hit me.

The car in front of me is turning and I follow it as closely as I can without hitting it: I have to be within a few feet of it just to see my headlights pick up and reflect back off of the car's trunk and rear bumper. This situation is growing more and more dangerous by the second, and yet I can't just stop my car here in the middle of the street and wait for better visibility. Talk about being between a rock and a hard place, I'm in one now, and a dangerous one to boot!

I've counted the intersections and I know which street I'm on, Twohig Street, and just a half a block away is the entrance to the rear parking lot of Sears, Roebuck and Company. I believe that if I can just creep along as close as I can to the car in front of me that I will, hopefully, and with lots of luck, be able to make out the entrance to the parking lot; I will turn into the parking lot, if I can see to dodge the parked cars, and then I will park there and sit in my car until the rain lets up enough to be able to drive safely. I occasionally lean across my front seat and try to obtain a fleeting glimpse of the cars that are angle parked on the sides of the streets. I can't see well enough to determine if there are any empty parking spaces for me to try and blindly maneuver into, so the Sears parking lot sounds like my best bet. I realize that I simply cannot keep driving. It's way too dangerous.

Once more I lean across my front seat toward the passenger window, desperate to get just a glimpse of where the parked cars are on the street, and also desperately trying to see the entrance to the parking lot while at the same time trying to keep an eye on the car that's only a few inches in front of me so that I don't rear-end it when suddenly, and I do mean suddenly, without any warning whatsoever the fierce, driving, blinding rain...stops.

Now I don't mean that the rain begins to lessen; and I don't mean that the rain has now begun to gradually decrease in intensity. No: literally one second ago I was experiencing the worst downpour I've ever seen in my lifetime, a deluge so bad that I could not see the end of the hood of my own car and now, *one second later,* there is not one bit of water falling from the sky. There is, suddenly, no rain at all, anywhere.

I reach up and turn my windshield wipers off and I stare out my windshield at the cloudy skies and the street and the cars in front of me and I look at the buildings and the signs; there's not so much as a mist hitting my windshield. I look in my rearview mirrors and see the street behind me, the cars behind me. *Perfect* visibility has instantly returned, although the skies are still overcast with dark clouds, and that visibility lets me see where I am: the car in front of me is perfectly visible to me and I can see the man sitting inside of it; I can see the rear corner of the Sears building and I'm almost at the entrance to the parking lot; I look ahead of me and there's perfect visibility as far as the eye can see; I glance into my rearview mirror again and as far as the eye can see...perfect visibility. This is passing strange.

As I'm sitting there taking all of this in and also wondering why traffic isn't moving I become aware that the cars that are eastbound on Twohig Street are swerving into my westbound lane, and a cacophony of blaring horns is warning of impending collisions as the drivers in my lane with virtually no room to maneuver try to swerve away. I wonder aloud, "What in the hell?" And then the tableau grows stranger still: cars come to stops at odd angles to avoid hitting other cars; I can see people frantically rolling their car windows down and pointing; doors of cars are flying open and the cars' occupants are spilling out into the street. People are waving wildly, yelling, pointing up at the sky in the direction of the Sears building. Everyone's gone mad!

And then it dawns on me...*oh, hell.* The reason everyone is exhibiting this behavior suddenly becomes, in my mind, crystal clear to me, and it explains all of the super-weird weather, the sudden start and stop of the torrential downpour of rain, and may possibly even explain my experience with the strange, supernatural cloud: everyone is pointing because the sudden calm has been caused by the impending touchdown of a killer tornado, maybe even an F5, and as it flows down from the angry skies the people up ahead have seen it and they're all in a blind panic.

In spite of my sudden feeling of dread I steel my nerves and I force myself to look up in the direction to which everyone's pointing, expecting to see a whirling mass of tornadic doom—Damn it...I'm too *young* to die!—and instead I'm greeted by the sight of a shiny metallic looking disc which is hovering maybe a hundred feet or less above the rear corner of the Sears building.

I literally perform a cartoon-style eye-rub, but when I look back up the UFO is still there, hovering silently. There is no smoke, no flame, and no noise. Just this shiny metallic disc, which I estimate to be about thirty to fifty feet in diameter, sitting there in the air...destroying my belief system.

I have had so many concrete paranormal and psychic experiences in my young life that I have almost come to take them for granted, but *I don't believe in UFOs!*

I look back down at the street, and people are pointing up at it, gesturing, talking animatedly. I grab the door handle to open up my car door and get out too when two things happen: the UFO appears to glide toward us slightly and then, very slowly and smoothly, a low cloud comes up from behind the UFO and covers it, and the *second* that the cloud covers the UFO the rain is *instantly back with all of its former intensity!* One second there's not a drop of moisture in the air, and literally the next second I can hardly see beyond the hood of the car.

Traffic quickly begins to crawl again (What else are we gonna do? We can't all just sit there in the street.) and lo and behold the car in front of me makes the turn into the Sears parking lot. I decide that I'm going to follow this man even if I hit his car, and when he parks I'm going to confront him and make him tell me what he just saw. I still can't believe my eyes, and I want to converse with someone else about this incredible sighting and verify that I wasn't hallucinating.

He parks, and I park right beside him, but before I can shift my transmission into park and turn my car off I see his dome light come on, glowing in the darkening gloom as he opens his car door and dashes out into the torrent of rain, heading across the parking lot and toward the rear entrance to Sears. I must act fast; I cannot let him get away! Fortunately I'm young and lithe and sure on my feet and as fast as a damn gazelle. I burst out of my car and immediately I am soaked to the bone by the pelting cold rain. The rain hits me with such stinging ferocity that it hurts my bare arms and I have to squint and shield my eyes to try and see well enough to make a run for the store but I make it, and there, standing just inside in the store's small vestibule, is the fellow who occupied the automobile in front of me. He's standing there as still as a stone with his head bowed; he's dripping water, and so am I. His eyeglasses are beaded with rain that he hasn't even bothered to wipe off yet. I walk around to stand close in front of him, and in a moment he realizes that I'm there and he looks up at me.

I ask him: *"Did you see what I just saw?"*

He stares at me for a bit. And then he answers. "Yeah, but I damn sure ain't gonna tell nobody." And with that he sidesteps me and walks briskly into the store.

I do not follow him. I realize that I have intruded as far into his life as he will allow me to. And I understand his statement, too: in the seventies, and especially in West Texas, people tend to regard you as being tetched in the head if you mention a belief in or supposed encounter with anything that smacked of the paranormal, much less a UFO.

So I stand there for a moment longer, chilled and dripping rainwater, my mind in a whirl. One of my major belief systems has just been destroyed. And then, with the storm still raging outside, I turn and take the steps down into the basement, to the sporting goods department. And around a half hour to an hour later, when the storm has finally abated enough to drive, I leave the Sears store and walk cautiously to my car, glancing around at the sky. I drive home without further incident, my mind still in a whirl.

I probably looked at one of the finest collections of sporting goods in the town of San Angelo that day and I can't tell you about one single item that I saw. The only thing I saw was that UFO. I couldn't get it out of my mind's eye. And I remember it to this day just as vividly as if it had happened only yesterday, and whenever I return to San Angelo I make it a point to go downtown to the old Sears building, which became home to the Tom Green County Public Library, and regardless of whether it's clear or overcast I turn my eyes to the sky over the building, and every time...I carry a camera.

Interlude: Unlike those who claim to know exactly what UFOs are and where they come from and who they belong to I did not jump on that particular bandwagon. I have formulated no theories because I haven't yet discovered a way to formulate a theory that makes any practical sense. This much I know: they exist. I have seen many others since that initial sighting. I have no idea whose they are or what they are. And until I obtain some hard evidence of whom the UFOs belong to and for what purposes they are here, I will abstain from formulating what can only be a half-cocked opinion based on assumption. There's enough of that kind of thinking that litters the paranormal landscape already, and I refuse to add my mental garbage to it.

And then, *what in the world was that cloud?* And what was its connection to the UFO, if any? I have an upcoming story about Tropical Storm Fay and a weird cloud I encountered during that time period too. I've also become aware of the concept of "intelligent storms." I wonder if that strange cloud that I encountered so many years ago may have been my first encounter with some type of an intelligent storm. But now let's jump decades ahead again to my sweet Florida home.

Our beautiful house has a lanai which looks into our back yard and the beautiful woods behind our home and our house also has a screened in courtyard which offers a different view of the sky and respite from Florida's Pit Bull-like mosquitoes which inflict some of the most painful, itchiest, longest lasting bites that I've ever suffered.

There is a door from the courtyard into the garage, and while I'm sitting in the courtyard if I open that door I can glance over at my beloved Melissa as she leans patiently on her kickstand, awaiting our next adventure together.

I love twilight, especially evening twilight, and as the night deepens and darkness enfolds me like a comforting blanket all of my senses feel more alive. The starry night has always held a fascination for me, even when I was a small child, and I never tire of watching the stars come out.

Most enjoyable is to ride my bike at night. It's much more dangerous, yes: even with reflective gear I'm still more difficult for other motorists to see, and road hazards are less visible to me than during the day, and of course there's the ever present danger of wild animals, especially deer, bounding out of the darkness and onto a collision course with me.

But the absolutely delicious and mystical feelings that riding at night evokes is worth the added risk. And I also ask the Other Side to give me extra special protection as I ride through the inky blackness, and they always have. Thanks, guys.

When sitting outside at night I will usually listen to some music, and I will always have a generous amount of cold alcoholic beverages. My favorite drinks are cold bottles of Budweiser beer and several glasses of Ezra Brooks whiskey on the rocks. Ah, whiskey: from the Irish *uisce beatha* & Scottish Gaelic *uisge beatha,* meaning, literally, water of life. I love it!

It's a standing joke with some of my friends that my nighttime visions are encouraged by my consumption of alcohol, whiskey in particular. Let's address that.

I have drunk heavily since I was eighteen years old, when that became the legal drinking age in Texas. Whatever your feelings about alcohol may be, this has been my experience: my biological family is a family of *heavy* drinkers; I cannot overemphasize that word, heavy. None of us has ever had a wreck because of being intoxicated. None of us has ever had a DWI/DUI conviction that I am aware of. And as far as I know none of us has ever gone to jail or lost a job because of our alcohol use.

I never forget a night before. I don't get sick or throw up. I never have hangovers. I can drink as much or as little as I desire; I sometimes go weeks or months without drinking. I sometimes drink daily for weeks or months.

I also have a gift that I'm not sure that the rest of my biological family enjoys, but I can mix any amount of any kind of liquor or beer and not be sick as a result. Additionally I can eat *any* foods and drink any other liquids I desire while I'm imbibing and not suffer any gastric disturbances. It's nice, because I like to drink, and I like to eat.

I just had my liver function checked and the doc said I have the liver function of a healthy twenty year old. Long may I live! So alcohol does not impair my ability to judge what I see in the same way that it might affect others who are not able to enjoy it like I am.

Anyway, while I'm sitting outside enjoying my libations and my music I enjoy watching the night sky. We live close to a small airport, so the little planes are puttering around our neighborhood through the night sky, their lights blinking and winking, and of course I will see the lights, way up high, of the occasional large airliner as it wings its way somewhere through the darkness.

Now if you've spent your life outdoors–both in the daytime and the nighttime, as I have–you learn to fairly accurately judge the sizes, shapes, and distances of objects that you observe. So I can judge the approximate distance and whereabouts of a small plane in the sky as it flies far north of my position as opposed to one that's nearby as it enters its landing pattern to approach the airport.

I can look up at those large airliners winging their ways through the darkness, and I can judge where they are in relation to the small planes down low and close to me, and where those airliners are in relation to the vast distance of the stars high above them. I, or anyone else, can make a reasoned judgment of the distances and sizes of these objects as they routinely fly around the skies, whether it's day or night.

And if you've sat outside enough and watched planes at night you know that when they turn their landing lights on it's not a UFO...it's a plane turning on its landing lights. If you see an object moving slowly through the skies and you look carefully, even if you can't hear engine noise, you can see the plane's blinking lights and you realize that it's not a UFO...it's a plane.

So I'm sitting outside one deliciously dark night around Thanksgiving, and I'm enjoying my first bottle of beer and my first glass of whiskey, and I'm watching the small planes buzz around the dark sky and I'm enjoying watching the twinkling stars and the planet Venus is off to my right; I'm facing roughly north and Venus is roughly east to me and big and round and bright. I know it's not a UFO; it's friggin' Venus. I *get it,* skeptics.

When the small planes are close enough to me if I listen carefully I can hear their engine noise. Their blinking lights are plainly visible in the darkness as they coast along against the backdrop of stars.

I'm enjoying this dark tableau when suddenly, in my peripheral vision off to my right, toward Venus, this bright, steadily glowing orange orb comes flying through the sky moving toward the north. As it catches my attention I look at it as it flies by Venus. As big and bright as Venus is in the sky that's how big and bright this object appears to be, but I can tell from its proximity that it is about as close to me as the small planes flying around. But this orange orb emits no sound, nor does it blink, nor does it have any blinking lights. It also seems to be almost translucent. Now it's got my full attention.

I don't have any music playing at the moment, so I can listen carefully. There is no noise of any kind that emanates from this steadily glowing orb. It cruises through the sky at about the same altitude that the small low-flying planes do and passes in front of my field of vision as it moves now in a more westerly direction. It's close to me.

"Son of a bitch," I mutter, "that's a friggin' UFO!"

I have read that some people claim that they have been able to send mental commands to a UFO and to get a response: "Stop flying. Hover. Now ascend slightly. Blink a light at me."

What the hell; why not? So I send out not just a mental command to this UFO, but a verbal one as well: "Hey! If you can hear me, stop!" The UFO is directly in front of my field of vision now, and it stops. *Holy crap.* It hovers there for a brief moment and then slightly reverses direction. This is cool.

And then it performs a maneuver that I don't know that I can adequately describe. I know one thing for sure, that I cannot convey to you how flabbergasted I am when I see this maneuver and neither can I convey to you how deeply this experience has affected me to this day. Here's what happens.

Imagine that an object the size of a small plane–say a Cessna Skyhawk–is flying close enough to you so that you can hear its engine noise and clearly see its blinking lights and if it were all lit up you could clearly see all of the plane and it would look about as big in the sky as Venus does when she's large and bright, or the plane might appear to be even closer to you. Anyway if it were daylight you would definitely be able to clearly see the plane in the sky, and maybe even be able to discern some of its markings. It's that close.

Now imagine how the distant blinking lights of those big airliners look as they cruise way up high through the night sky.

What happens in *less* than one second's time is that this glowing orb ascends to that height in the sky! It remains steady there for a moment, its brightness just a little more than that of the airliner's lights as they traverse the heavens.

It remains at that altitude for a brief moment and then, again in less than one second's time, it abruptly shoots up into the stars. It moves in an easterly direction for a tiny bit and then, again, in less than one second's time, it ascends into the inky blackness of the universe and disappears from sight. Even as I write this I have to pause for a moment just now; witnessing this event has made a large and lasting impact on me.

I don't know what the object was. I know it wasn't a planet, or a plane, or a helicopter, or a rocket, or a Chinese Lantern floating through the heavens.

I don't know if it's "ours," "theirs," or maybe something developed by some military: our own, or someone else's. What I *do* know is that the performance characteristics of this thing are absolutely ungodly. Whatever it is, whosoever it is, it's absolutely frightening to think that such a thing exists that can apparently virtually elude the laws of time and space while hiding the revelation of its true existence from all of us.

My fervent hope used to be that we would all become aware of the truth about UFOs before I pass from this Earth. Now I'm sometimes not so sure that I want to know. After all, no less a scientific luminary than Stephen Hawking has stated, in reference to extraterrestrial contact, that "If aliens visit us, the outcome would be much as when Columbus landed in America, which didn't turn out well for the Native Americans."

# Epilogue

Since that one incredible experience I have had several others. For a couple of years I have experienced a virtual UFO flap here, and the odd thing is that the craft all seem to vanish in that same part of the sky. I have not seen any that have ascended in stages as dramatically as that one did; most seem to fly into that part of the sky and simply vanish from sight. These craft vanish when it's a completely clear, starry night which is devoid of clouds.

I have called for my wife to come out and she has observed them too. She has even had a few sightings of her own that I've not been privy to.

All of these have been nighttime sightings, as opposed to the daylight sighting when I experienced my very first UFO, although I did have one other daylight sighting when I was riding on a train, just as it left the station in Chicago. There was a very large "inverted pie plates" craft hovering low in a clear blue sky as the train pulled out. I didn't even bother to ask any of the other passengers to look; at the time, *I* didn't want to be thought of as tetched in the head.

# Update: July, 2016, Florida

Another UFO sighting, this one moving slowly from a northerly to southerly direction. I had woken up from a sound sleep to go to the bathroom and when I came back I spied it out of my bedroom window. I watched it until it went out of sight behind the cover of some trees, shrugged, and went back to bed.

# CHAPTER VI

# People of the Owl

MELISSA IS PARKED on the opposite shore, chained to a tree, and she has her disc lock/alarm in place and activated.

I am returning to her on the very same passenger ferry which took me away from her to begin with. The word "bear" jolts me out of my state of contemplation.

The only other passenger with me on the ferry has asked the park ranger, who is captaining the boat, a question about bears and their question for the ranger has, in turn, attracted my full attention.

I ask the ranger: "So, do you have any bears on the island?"

He grins and rolls his eyes. "Boy–*do we have bears!*" He then proceeds to regale us with a brief account of the many bears on the island and the mischief which they cause. I ask him how they get onto the island, and he informs me that bears are not only excellent swimmers, but excellent *long-distance* swimmers, too. The relatively short hop across this body of water is not even a minor challenge for the furry paddlers.

The ranger and the passenger continue the bear talk, but I don't listen; I lapse back into my contemplation of the dramatic events that have occurred over the past several hours…

I park Melissa in the grass, sliding a side stand plate underneath her side stand so that she won't tip over in the soft soil, and then I chain her to a nearby tree and attach her disc lock/alarm.

I walk to the dock and wait for the ferry as instructed. The ferry will take me across the river to Hontoon Island. Native Americans were its first inhabitants, and one of the things that I learn about one of the tribes is that they utilized a large owl totem: they were known as the people of the owl. In a few hours' time this bit of knowledge will become both more significant *and* more important to me than I can possibly even begin to imagine now.

The ferry arrives and the park ranger captaining it exchanges pleasantries with me as I come aboard, and then we're heading across to the island. It's a beautiful sunny summer day; that fact will also become more significant and important to me than I can possibly imagine now as I enjoy the leisurely pace of the ferry as it glides across the water.

When we disembark I chat with the ranger awhile and I tell him my main reason, ostensibly, for coming to the island: to hike to the shell mound, a huge mound of discarded snail shells which is the preserved evidence of the Indians' staple food; but the real reason I have come is to allow my psychic senses to connect with the energies here, past and present, and see what the Other Side might have to tell me about this place and the people who lived here so long ago.

The ranger gives me the lay of the land and shows me the ranger station, the restrooms, the soda and snack machines and the water fountain; yet another item in my growing list of things which will become ominously important to me this day. And for all of my psychic powers that I possess I fail to make a connection with any of it, even after I take a long drink of the cold water from the fountain. Bear with me, please; you'll soon understand.

I obtain some brochures about the history of the island and the ranger points me in the direction of the path I will follow to the shell mound and bids me enjoy, and I'm off. The brochure states that the shell mound is a leisurely walk of about an hour and I regularly hike such distances and more. It's a fine sunny day and warming quickly, and I feel good and I'm in good spirits, and I'm looking forward to this hike and to both the psychic and physical exploration, each of which is an adventure in its own right.

The island is beautiful, and I feel myself becoming immersed in Nature's glory as I begin the hike. Today, as is so often the case in many of Florida's state parks, I have the trail, and the forest, to myself. I don't meet with another soul. This will also play into the events to come.

But right now I'm enjoying the beauty of the scenery so much that I almost don't notice some type of energy or presence that is closing in on me; I suddenly become aware that this presence is to the rear of me and to my right hand side, but before I can even turn my head to look it's upon me: there is something in my peripheral vision at about my height, at my eye level. Not more than a few feet away from me a *large owl* glides by me so close that the feathers of its left wingtip almost brush my cheek and I can feel the rush of air on my shoulder and face!

I catch my breath as the owl dips down slightly in its flight path and continues to glide over the hiking path in front of me as I walk, and then it suddenly swoops up into the air toward a tree, making a pivoting turn in the air to land on a branch facing me as I walk toward it. A tree, once again, on the left hand side of the trail.

Wow: *The people of the owl!* I'm on the island of the people of the owl, and out of the blue here comes this huge owl and flies by close enough for me to touch it, and then it glides down the path in front of me, and then comes to a rest on a branch facing me, and this bird locks eyes with me as I walk the path toward it and it does not look away, not once.

I stop and stand underneath the tree branch that this magnificent bird sits upon (Or is it a spirit sitting up there in that tree?) and I speak to it with respect and awe, and I tell this magnificent bird that I know a little of the history of the island and that a significant part of that history was lived out there by the people of the owl, and I thank the owl for its presence, for the entire experience, and I ask the owl to impart to me whatever knowledge, wisdom, guidance, and protection that it is able to provide to me. I stand there and I talk to the owl for a long time, and not *once* do its eyes ever leave mine. I finally tell it that I'm going on to the shell mound and that I will always remember and cherish this experience, and I leave the owl with a blessing.

I tingle with excitement for the rest of my walk. I try to tune into whatever energies or spirits may communicate with me, but I'm so excited by this incredible experience with the owl that I'm having trouble focusing my psychic senses.

The rest of my senses are fine, though...I'm becoming aware that it's getting hot. The sun is beating down and the air is growing thick with Florida's notorious and dangerous heat and humidity.

But so far I feel fine, and I'm so enervated by the experience with the owl that I continue my hike, enjoying the scenery, and I finally reach the end of the trail...the famous shell mound. On the top of the mound there is a bench which overlooks the forest, and I'm grateful for the opportunity to sit and rest my legs. I also take this opportunity to try and tune in psychically and see if the Other Side provides any revelations or insights about these peoples to me, but I don't seem to get much of anything beyond a general understanding that their life was lived here. Perhaps I will have to return time and again in order to achieve a psychic breakthrough.

There is camping on the island...how I would love to spend several nights here, wandering freely and interacting with the energies and the spirits; and maybe...the owls?

After a good amount of time has passed I reluctantly stand up to return through the forest to the ranger station, over an hour away. I feel nostalgic and I don't want to leave. I'm at home in the woods with this isolation and serenity.

As I begin my return hike I start to have an unsettled feeling.

I know from past experience that once I get really overheated I can't usually cool down except by soaking in a tub of cold water, or literally sitting in front of an air conditioner for a long period of time. I know these things because I used to run long distances and bicycle long distances in the West Texas heat, and I've always been prone to heat exhaustion. It doesn't happen every single time I'm out in the heat; I have to pay attention to my body and kind of go by how I'm feeling that day. Well, this day I thought that I had listened to my body; I always give myself kind of a psychic checkup before I venture out, and I might have been okay today if I had prepared with that one essential ingredient that helps a person to survive in the heat, the one thing that I had failed to make the essential connection with earlier: water. I didn't take any water with me and now it's getting close to noon; noon in the Florida heat. Florida, the place where I went to Navy boot camp and it gets so hot and humid that they would fly a black flag on the flagpole and that meant that it was literally physically dangerous for normal, healthy recruits to do anything except walk because of the danger of heat exhaustion or even heatstroke.

And now here I am without a speck of water, and since I've had multiple bizarre health issues ever since I was a child I've never been a normal, healthy recruit to begin with, and suddenly and without warning I'm feeling dangerously overheated and I still have almost an hour's walk to the ranger station and there's not another soul in sight to help me if anything goes wrong. Indeed, if I were to pass out on this trail it could conceivably be hours or even days before anyone found me. Not good!

I begin to walk slower so as to try not to build up any more excess body heat, but I'm not sure that's a helpful tactic either: the longer I'm in the sun and out in the heat, the more my body temperature will rise whether I'm exerting or not.

I'm by the river, but I don't dare drink the unfiltered river water; splashing it on me to cool myself down lasts all of a few seconds before the water evaporates and I feel the heat boring into me again like a laser beam; and with all of the gators and gator attacks that we have in Florida there's no way I'm stripping down and plunging into the river to cool myself off!

My cell phone. I can call the ranger station for help if I need to, if things get really bad. *If* I can get a signal out here, and *if* I can get hold of directory assistance and get the number for the ranger station, and *if*...ah, hell; all of that's irrelevant: my cell phone's battery is dead. Man...I *know* better than this. I have hunted and fished and camped and hiked and I've been an outdoorsman all of my life and I know how to take the necessary precautions when going into the wild, and I've usually done so. How could things have gone so wrong today? It's almost as if potential catastrophe after potential catastrophe has been deliberately set into motion...

I could be in real trouble here. It won't do any good for anyone to find me on the trail if I'm brain-damaged from a massive heatstroke; or dead. *Spirit, help me.*

I round a corner in the path, and I look up at the tree and it's been over an hour since I first passed this way but the exact same owl is still sitting there on the exact same branch in the exact same position and is staring down at me. This is incredible and astonishing.

I stop and I speak aloud and I tell the owl my plight. I apologize for being stupid. I tell the owl that I know that Nature does not forgive fools, nor treat them lightly.

I continue to address the owl aloud. "But can you please help me somehow? I've made a mistake, a serious one, I know. I should have thought to bring water, but for some god-awful reason I didn't think ahead, and now I'm paying the price, and I'm starting to feel really bad physically, and I know that there might not be another single person that hikes this trail today, and I need help, please."

The owl says nothing to me either physically or psychically, but it never averts its eyes from mine. After I've plead my case the best that I can I bless the owl again for showing itself to me, and I leave it with a serious benediction: "Please help me and look after me if you can, and if I've made a really stupid mistake today that leads to my demise, then, as I've read that the Native Americans used to say,"–and here I pause to take in my magnificent surroundings...the water, the blue sky dotted here and there by puffy white clouds, the awe-inspiring forest–and then I say it too, and I mean it: "then this is a good day to die."

I'm not being melodramatic. I realize the very real possibility that I could have a heat stroke and keel over right here on this trail, miles from help, and that it could be hours or maybe even days before anyone hiked out here and found me.

Oh god, will Marjorie be mad at me!

I wave goodbye to the owl and I trudge forward at a slow, even pace. In Florida it's usually so humid that sweat doesn't evaporate much, so sweating doesn't provide that much of a cooling effect. But then I notice something that *really* worries me: my sweat output is decreasing, a sure sign that I'm headed toward heat exhaustion or possibly even heatstroke, and I still have a long, long way to go to the ranger station.

I begin to focus on my breathing and I begin to meditate, using everything I've learned about mind over matter to work on controlling my body temperature and helping it to combat the effects of the heat.

The temperature continues to rise; both the air's...and mine.

I'm feeling so hot and dry, and while I'm normally hyperaware of everything that goes on around me (with the odd exception of the owl being upon me before I was cognizant of it) right this moment I'm so focused on using every psychic technique that I can utilize to stay alive that I once again fail to notice the strong physical presence behind me until it feels like it's almost upon me.

You ever suddenly become aware of a physical presence behind you? You *know* beyond any shadow of a doubt that there is a person behind you. You can feel their presence, their energy, their life force. I suddenly get that feeling. There is a person behind me. *Oh thank god.*

All of a sudden my psychic senses click into high gear and without even turning to look I know that this is a large male presence behind me, and he's close, not more than 15 or 20 feet away. Strange, I didn't pass any other hikers on the trail while walking either direction, but maybe it's one of the rangers and he was working off the trail out in the forest, and now he's coming back in. Oh, thank god... maybe he's got some water!

I turn with a smile of relief on my face and I meet, face to face...a large man. A large Native American Indian *spirit!* He is there as clear as day. He looks at me with a mixture of pity and scorn, and then he slowly shakes his head at me.

"I know...I know," I mutter. I'm a fool today; he knows it, and I know it.

Suddenly a thought springs unbidden into my mind: the owl *was* a spirit and he heard my plea and he has sent this Indian spirit to me as an answer...the Other Side knew that I would make this foolhardy trek today and that I would meet my demise right here on this trail. Right here and right now on this very spot I will keel over and this Native American spirit has come to cross me over to the Other Side. *Marjorie is going to be so damn mad at me.*

Instead he speaks to me. "Come on," he tells me, "I'm going to walk you safely out of the forest."

You mean I'm not going to die here today? I'm going to be alright? I'm so full of gratitude that I nearly tear up, but I must be strong in the presence of so powerful a spirit.

*"Thank you!"* It's all I can manage. I suspect that somehow he knows the rest.

I turn back around to resume my hike back to the ranger station and I can feel this powerful spirit's presence directly behind me, and suddenly he places one of his large, muscular hands on my left shoulder, and I can literally, physically feel his hand on me as he guides me forward. And then, from out of nowhere, a cooling breeze begins to caress me. I begin to cool down, in spite of the soaring temperature, and this Indian spirit marches me safely out of the forest.

He removes his hand from my shoulder and I turn to face him. I'm close enough to the ranger station that I will make it safely now. Before the Indian turns to leave me he soundly reprimands me for my stupidity, and I, with immense gratitude, thank him again for literally saving my life.

I'm at the ranger station, and I drink copious amount of cold water and I splash it over my face and head, repeatedly. I purchase a soda, and drink it. And then I drink some more cold water. It takes me a long time before I finally stop feeling woozy and nauseated.

I finally feel good enough to take the ferry back across the river to Melissa, and I know that once I get on the road the windblast will help to cool me down even more.

On the ferry I fall into a deep contemplation as I think about myself out there alone on Hontoon Island, miles away from the ranger station, and not another soul in sight; the powerful visitations from the owl and the Indian, and his dramatic rescue of me. *Hontoon Island, where the bears love to roam;* and unprovoked bear attacks, I've read lately, are on the rise. Wow...I've been saved from more than the heat today.

Before I even disembark the ferry I'm putting together in my mind a list of items to bring in a backpack the next time I venture into the forest, and bottles of water and/or a canteen tops the list. A backup battery for my cell phone is another item I won't do without again. And also a can of...*bear spray.*

Why would I take these precautions when I have just experienced such a miraculous supernatural rescue? Wouldn't the Other Side come to my aid in such a fashion again? Well, there's an old saying in spiritual work which surely applies here: "The Shaman may have given you a charm, but he did not tell you to sleep in the middle of the crossroads."

In other words, we're supposed to use our God-given common sense; and we're supposed to learn from our mistakes so that we don't repeat them.

I disembark the ferry, thank the ranger, and walk the short distance to Melissa. I unlock her and fire her up, and I wave goodbye to the island. Because of my shortsightedness in an area where I know better I've had a really close call today, and I literally owe my life to the owl, and to this Native American spirit who walked me out of the forest, providing supernatural cooling for me on the way. Thank you for hearing my cry for help, and for answering.

I have been saved by the kindness of the people of the owl. I will not forget.

It's not the first time that those on the Other Side have literally saved my life; and it will not be the last. I am deeply grateful and appreciative of that fact.

For all of our experience and knowledge, and technology, both the Powers That Be and Mother Nature can very quickly remind us of who's really in charge. It's very easy for us to get in over our heads very quickly, while not even recognizing the potential danger that is stealthily creeping our way.

It's a difficult planet to live on: we're continually beset with earthquakes, fires, hurricanes, volcanic eruptions, tornadoes, lightning... and as it has been said, Nature is not human hearted (Lao Tzu).

Nature itself and natural things–plants, animals, weather–are seemingly not very keen to be overly accommodating to us. Tsunamis drown us by the hundreds without any apparent regret. Bears attack and kill hikers and campers and sometimes eat them without any apparent remorse. And while one plant may contain a beneficial curative to ease or heal our discomfort from some dread disease yet another plant, perhaps one that's even very similar in appearance, will kill us if ingested. And very little in nature comes with a clear warning label attached.

And so too, in spite of its loving guidance, the spiritual realm.

If we go into the unknown unprepared or should we dare to venture where we ought not to tread in the first place we may be left to our own devices, and hopefully the lesson learned is not our final one on this old Earth.

Maybe there is a lot of wisdom in the line from the poem, that "Fools rush in where angels fear to tread."

# Epilogue

Over the course of the next several weeks nearly everywhere I turn there is an abnormal abundance of owl-related items and experiences. The people of the owl are still watching over me. And to this very day I still pay them homage, thinking of them with fondness and gratitude for their rescue and for allowing me to still be here, safe and sound, to share this story with you.

Once again, brave warrior spirit, thank you for saving my life.

Valuable lessons learned, appreciated, and appropriated with gratitude.

Please help me to share this with others.

Amen.

CHAPTER **VII**

# Phantom Phone Calls

AH–THE SUN SHINES warmly on me as I sit on a bench in Riverdale Park which is located on the banks of the Saint John's River here in Florida.

Melissa, my motorcycle, is the only vehicle in the parking lot, and I'm the only human inhabitant of the park. I'm enjoying the solitude: my life is spent dealing with peoples' energies and problems on a daily basis, and I have to recharge my batteries just like everyone else does, and for me solitude and peace and quiet is one of the best ways for me to do that, and thankfully Florida contains a bountiful number of places where I can find that needed escape.

As I sit here I'm watching a barge make its way downriver; eventually its wake reaches the shoreline where I'm sitting and it gets me to thinking about waves of all kinds, not just watery ones, and it boggles my mind for me to think that I can pull the cell phone out of my pocket and wirelessly send waves through the air that will accurately transmit the sound of my particular voice, and I can make a call to someone right here in this very town or I can call a buddy of mine who lives clear across the world in Oslo, Norway, all while sitting right here on this very bench, and whether I'm making a call to someone who's several hundred feet away or several thousand miles away we can talk to each other in real time. If that isn't magic, I don't know what is.

Didn't someone once say that technology is magic made visible?

Anyway, this train of thought eventually pulls into the Station of the Paranormal, and I get to thinking about people who have received phone calls from a lot farther away than Norway. It's well documented that many people have claimed to have received phone calls... from the dead.

In one instance I remember reading about a man who answered his home phone and had a pleasant 15 minute conversation with a friend of his with whom he was not in much regular contact. After saying goodbye and hanging up the man's wife enquired as to the identity of the caller, and the man explained that it was their old friend so-and-so and wasn't it nice that he had thought of them and had called to catch up. His wife agreed and they discussed the banalities of the conversation and, probably due to consulting a TV guide or program schedule or just, as people routinely do, they checked the time and also took note of the time of the call.

Imagine their shock when a mutual friend called to inform them of the passing of the man who had called them...who had called them on the exact day and at the exact time that he had just expired while lying in a hospital bed in a city far away.

I mull this over and while I don't believe that I have *received* any phone calls from the Other Side I recall an incident where one of my outgoing calls may have been *intercepted* by someone on the Other Side. I'm glad the sunshine's warm, because when I recall the details of this story it gives me chills even now; it didn't scare me, but it was one of the creepier paranormal encounters that I've had. You'll see what I mean as we return to my younger days once more and travel back in time to my old home place in Texas.

I have a dear and treasured friend named Bill that I hang out with frequently. We enjoy each other's company and we have a lot in common: I'm an artist, and so is he. He is a hunter and loves guns and knives, and so do I. We both share a fondness for good food, beautiful women, lots of booze, crappy movies rated one and a half stars or less, a couple of favorite bars that we both frequent, and Enya.

Another of the things that we have in common is that we like to pull pranks on each other: at a bar he once tossed a lit match onto me when I wasn't looking and actually started a small fire in my lap that I had to douse by pouring a glass of water on it. Yes, we are sometimes a handful to deal with. We even have a nickname: when people see us coming they shake their heads, roll their eyes, and proclaim, "Oh, god, here comes the Toxic Twins!" When we're out carousing together people tend to be a little bit leery and somewhat wary when it comes to sitting close to us; I wonder why?

And one of *my* favorite irritants is to wait until I'm reasonably sure that Bill has just nodded off to sleep and then I will call his house, wake him up, and then blather to him until he curses me and hangs up on me.

Naturally if you're going to make a habit of tormenting someone in this manner you want to enjoy convenience with it: I have Bill's number programmed into my cordless phone on speed dial. (This is obviously before the common use of cell phones.)

So on this particular evening, a short time ago, I have called Bill using the speed dial function on my phone. We chatted briefly and then he informed me that he was giving it up for the night. We said our goodbyes and I started my stopwatch function on my wristwatch. I've been watching TV and as I glance down at my watch I see the elapsed time has been about thirty minutes since our call; perfect! Bill should either be asleep or just dozing off.

Oh, I guess I should mention that there is *some* consideration to my dastardly behavior: Bill is a widower, and lives alone. But aren't I worried that my prank call will one night interrupt some coital behavior? That would be even better if it did, but I am aware of one of Bill's particular quirks, and that is the inalterable fact that Bill never brings a woman back to his house; never. We've discussed it; Bill's explained his reasoning; it's a rule that I've never known him to violate.

So, grinning like the proverbial opossum that's eating briars, I pick up my phone and hit the speed dial number for Bill's phone, pushing the exact same button that I had used earlier in the evening to call him the first time.

Set *my* lap on fire, huh buddy? Revenge is sweet: get ready for my merciless harassment. There's two or three rings and then the sound of a receiver picking up and a *woman's* voice says lazily, "Hello?"

For a moment I can't speak. I quickly pull the phone away from my head and double check that I pressed the right button; I did. *What in the hell?*

I'm caught completely off guard, and I actually begin to stammer. "I'm sorry; I was trying to reach Bill. Is he there?"

"No." She speaks slowly; softly; sleepily; lazily. Weirdly.

"Has he gone out?" I ask.

"No. There's no Bill over here," she says in her slightly husky, lazy, dreamy, weird voice.

Man–what in the hell is going on?! Is Bill pranking *me?* But the odd way in which she has responded is my first clue that this may not be a prank: she said, "There's no Bill *over* here."

"I'm really sorry," I say. "Is this–?" and I recite Bill's number, the number that I know without a doubt is the one that I dialed.

"No, it isn't," she says.

*But I know beyond any shadow of a doubt that's the number I just dialed. The number is programmed into my speed dial. That means I can't have misdialed! I know I've dialed Bill's number, so where in the heck is Bill? And who is this woman?*

Quickly I rev up my psychic senses. I *know* that I will be able to discern whether or not this is Bill pranking me by having some woman there to answer the phone in expectation of my call. I send out my psychic radar wave, and when the return comes I almost wish that I hadn't done it, for in a split second I know the absolute truth, and it is this: I have *dialed correctly* all right, but I'm pretty sure that I have not reached Bill's home. So *who* have I reached, and *where?*

Now this is before digital phone and all of these wonderful improvements that we enjoy today; this is back in the day when sometimes you could still tell that a call was long distance by the way it sounded and this call *sounds* like a long distance call, like I might have reached someone from overseas; or maybe even farther away...

The woman sounds like I have just woken *her* from sleep, but that isn't what's getting to me. What's creeping me out just a little bit is the quality of her voice. Her voice is deep and dreamy, but very strange sounding. I've talked to a lot of women, but no woman has ever sounded like this woman sounds. There is literally an otherworldly quality to her voice. And there is some weird quality to this call that I can't quite put my finger on, like perhaps I've reached another dimension or something. My psychic senses are all buzzing now; there is definitely something not quite right about this call.

And suddenly things get *really* bizarre: this is what the woman says to *me:* "This is John Russell, isn't it?"

Now my skin has goose bumps; I am completely taken aback; this call has just gone from strange to passing strange.

"Well, yes, it is," I stammer; "who is this, please?"

There's a brief pause before she speaks again. The call sounds, if that's possible, like it's becoming more distant, but at the same time there's an unusual clarity and I can hear her voice just fine. Her words remain clear and distinct.

"Hmm," she says, "so *you're* John Russell." A strange emphasis.

"Yes, I am, and I'm very sorry, but I don't know what number I've accidentally managed to reach and I apologize, but I don't recognize *your* voice. What number have I reached, and who is this and how do you know me?"

"So *this* is *John Russell.*" Again the strange emphasis. My freaky-weird meter is pegged.

"Yes. Please, who have I reached? I apologize again but I don't recognize your voice at all, and I wonder how you recognize my voice and seem to know me but yet I don't recognize your voice at all and I don't seem to know you? What's your name, please? Who is this?"

There is another pause, and then, instead of answering any of my questions, she says, "I'm sorry, I'm very tired now. I'm going to bed. Good night." She has drawn out the word "tired" and placed great emphasis on it, as if the call has almost literally drained her of all of her available energy.

And before I can say another word, she's hung up.

Oh, no-no-no-no-no! I'm not done with this whacky conversation! I immediately hit the exact same speed dial button that I had hit before...and *this* time I connect with, and wake, my old friend Bill.

Psychically I can tell that he is not "possumming," but that he truly was asleep and that I have just woken him. Nevertheless I ask: "Bill, have you been asleep up until now when I called. Did I just wake you up?" Yes. "Bill, this is important, and I'll explain it to you tomorrow, but is there a woman there with you? I have an important reason for asking and I'm being completely serious, so please, tell me the truth." No. "Between our last call tonight when we said good night and the one right now did I call you?" No. "Did your phone ring at all?" No. Bill thinks I have gotten way too drunk.

My mind's in such a whirl that I don't know what to think. Bill's bumfuzzled and wants to know what in the hell is going on, but I tell him that I'll see him tomorrow and that I'll explain everything then. Right now he's tired and sleepy and wants to go back to sleep, and I have to run this around in my mind for awhile and try to sort it out and make some sense out of it, and so I bid my buddy good night... again.

The next day I meet with Bill and I tell him everything. The paranormal scares the shit out of Bill. He doesn't want to talk about it. End of story. I'm left with this incredible psychic experience which involved this strange woman and Bill's telephone number, and I've got no one to talk to about it. Until now...with you.

I had never heard that mysterious woman's voice before, and I've never heard it since. However hers was a voice that I believe I could recognize to this day; I doubt I'll ever forget it due to its dreamy and slightly creepy qualities.

So who was this phantom woman? The only thing that I can surmise is that someone on the Other Side was able to intercept my call and that they somehow had the energy to hold a brief conversation with me; and here's the chilling part: it was someone who obviously *knew me;* and yet I did not know them.

Makes you wonder just who is keeping tabs on us from the Other Side, and for what reasons, huh?

I wonder: will I ever speak with the phantom woman again? And, more importantly: *who is she?*

# Epilogue

An odd thought crosses my mind from time to time: while Bill was passed out asleep did the spirit of his deceased wife answer my call? I don't know which the creepier thought is: that there may be someone on the Other Side who watched my developing friendship with her husband and managed to take my phone call to him while he was asleep, or that there is some phantom woman out there who knows me, or knows of me, and that she intercepted my call.

I sure would like to know which one it is.

I have had another experience with a ghostly phone call, this one from a deceased motorcycling buddy, but that's a story that we'll examine a little farther down the road.

First a little bit more about my dear old friend Bill. He's deceased now, but periodically visits me in my dreams. He was a good friend to me, and I miss him a lot. A too-long story that's meant to be told in another time and place, but long story short for a couple of years of my life I became homeless. Health issues precluded me from working at even the most menial of simple jobs; I had no money and no income; and I also had no means of transportation. Most frighteningly, I had no place to lay my head at night, no place to live. I was *homeless.* It was the most terrifying experience of my life!

Bill, my friend, an intensely private person, took me in. Into his home. Gave me a bedroom of my own. Fed me. And helped me to get back on my feet. It was a long process that tested my faith and Bill's patience, but we made it through and remained friends until Bill crossed over to the Other Side. It's something that I was always grateful for. And I still am. I still talk to Bill, and I tell him often that I appreciate what a powerful difference in my life his personal sacrifice made to me.

Now, as I mentioned earlier, Bill was literally scared to death of the paranormal…he acknowledged its reality…and he acknowledged my psychic gift…but he didn't want anything to do with either one of them.

Shortly after I moved in Bill once told me: "John, I believe that you have a genuine gift. I believe in everything that you do. But…if you sense, hear, feel, see, or whatever, *anything* here in this home…*I don't want to know about it!*"

Now the paranormal follows me like butterflies follow the nectar trail. Paranormal events on the physical realm are an almost daily occurrence with me…sometimes they're so "small" that most people wouldn't consider them significant but other times they can be very attention getting! So I asked the guys to please hold off on physical manifestations while Bill was home. Sometimes he would leave the house to run errands, or he would go out without me (we were still the best of drinking buddies but sometimes I felt too bad to go to the bars with him) and a few times he would go and visit an old army buddy or take some short vacation of several days or a week and leave me in charge of his home. It was a trust I never betrayed and I asked the guys to not betray this particular trust either. This is the conversation that I held with them.

"Guys, you know that nothing scares me. I get startled every now and then by these events the same as anyone would, but nothing ever truly frightens me, not at all. But Bill is scared to death by this stuff, and I've got to live here with him for awhile until I get back on my feet. So, will you please refrain from manifestations, especially noise-making, while Bill is home? You can do whatever you please when he's gone, but please, please behave when he's here."

You know, we make the false assumption that just because some-one shuffles off their mortal coil and transitions to life on the Other Side that they must suddenly become all wise, all knowing, and total-ly benign and angelic in nature. Ha! Not so. It's been my experience in communicating with those on the Other Side that we retain our memories, our personalities, and our sense of humor…intact. If your uncle was a horrible prankster here on this side, more than likely you can expect to experience your share of paranormal hijinks directed toward you from him while he's on the Other Side.

I've also learned that spirits, spirits that were never human, such as nature spirits, etc., may also possess a keen sense of humor and/or mischief. Bear this in mind as I continue my story.

So, for the most part, with the exception of a small noise here, and an item moved there, the guys behaved themselves.

Until one night while Bill and I were watching TV together.

Bill and I loved crappy movies rated 1-1/2 stars or less. Preferably with a lot of senseless violence, nudity, sex, cursing, and even those with a monster or supernatural element was okay as long as it met the other requirements.

Bill's house had an open floor plan from the small kitchen into the adjacent dining room and that was all open to and connected with the living room, where we sat watching TV.

We had found one of our ideal movies. I had told Bill when we began to watch that we had to find something else to view unless, within the first fifteen minutes of this movie, someone was killed, something scary and or violent happened, and someone had sex, preferably with a lot of mindless cursing thrown in. We hit the jack-pot! Within fifteen minutes of the start of this movie all of those things happened!

We each got a fresh bottle of beer and settled in to watch and enjoy.

We were maybe half an hour into the movie when, from the kitch-en which was only mere feet away, there came a clatter so loud that it sounded as if someone had stacked 10 or 15 cookie sheets together, climbed up to the top of a six foot tall ladder, and then dropped them onto the floor.

Bill was a good cook, and I was a good cook. And we both kept the kitchen clean after every meal that we made, so we both knew that there wasn't any errant thing in the kitchen that could possibly account for such a racket as the one we'd just heard.

I looked over at Bill, and he resolutely refused to remove his gaze from the TV screen. His hands were clenched so tightly into the arms of his soft recliner that his fingers were invisible!

"Bill?" I said.

"Yep."

"Didja hear that?" I asked.

"Yep."

"Ain't you gonna get up and go see what it was?"

"Nope."

Today, as I did then, I still laugh out loud thinking about Bill's reaction.

And of course there was nothing in the kitchen to account for such a racket. I guess the guys simply couldn't contain themselves any longer and had to act out just this once in such a dramatic fashion. They just had to have a little fun. At poor Bill's expense.

But Bill was a trooper about it. Although, for the rest of the night I had to be the one to get up and walk into the kitchen to get us each another beer.

# CHAPTER VIII

# Fay

FAY.

That was the name of the lady who breezed through Florida in August of 2008.

Growing up in Tornado Alley in West Texas I have survived tornadoes, but this is my first hurricane experience. A hurricane is basically a very slow moving giant tornado, so I am not looking forward to the possibility of such an event.

My wife and I attend to the basics to prepare for such an event: we stockpile non-perishable food, and lots and lots of water; we provide ourselves with several flashlights, spare bulbs and batteries, and battery-powered radios; we fill both bathtubs full of water; and we provide for ways to cook without power, such as Sterno, and charcoal briquettes to use in our barbecue grill. We also purchase a couple of camping cook sets to use on the grill or over the Sterno so that we won't ruin our good pots and pans, and we stock up on disposable knives, forks, spoons, plates, and glasses to cut down on the necessity of having to wash dishware in case we lose water for days on end as has happened to Florida's hurricane victims in the past. We make sure that we have a good supply of all of our necessary medications, and that there is plenty of food for our pets. We try to keep the gas tank in our car full, and we also plan in advance as to what we will do just in case we're given an order to evacuate.

And then we wait; and we hope and we pray for Fay to stay away. And Fay comes. She's not hurricane strength, but she is a record-setting tropical storm unlike anything Florida's seen before.

And she bumfuzzles everybody. The experienced weather fore-casters that we are watching every day on TV say that they have never seen a storm behave quite like Fay is behaving: you can't predict her. They say that she's moving, and suddenly she sits still. They say she's going east, and she veers west. They say she'll be out of the state soon, and she hangs around longer. Fay moves slowly over just about the whole state of Florida before all is said and done, but she doesn't move in one direction only, she moves up and back, and from side to side. And I begin to have really creepy feelings: Fay is sentient, intel-ligent, and self-aware; and she's looking for something.

It's taken me awhile to come around to this way of thinking that storms may be inhabited by beings of some type, or that maybe the storm itself is some form of intelligent life. Some American Indians held a similar belief, and as I begin to research this train of thought I discover that peoples around the world hold comparable ideolo-gies. Over the years, because of my paranormal experiences that are storm related (Remember that weird cloud I encountered when I had my first UFO experience?) I have come to embrace these beliefs as sensible possibilities: that storms may be inhabited by, or directed by, intelligent beings, and also I accept the possibility that the storm itself may somehow be a form of intelligence.

I know, it's pretty far out, isn't it? But when you've experienced what I have there's not too much left in life that strikes you as bizarre or unbelievable.

Anyway, you can research the idea for yourself, that storms may somehow be intelligent. It's an area that I plan to research more fully for myself.

So as Fay continues to hover over our fair state I allow myself the possibility that she's intelligent and that she's also here for a reason, and so I ask the Other Side, "What is that reason?"

And here's what they tell me: First, our entire state has been in a severe drought, and Fay has come to provide some much needed relief; which, through her rainfall, she does. (And proving that there's a yang for every yin she also produces a lot of flooding and related damage in the process.) Second, Fay is looking for something; something specific. When I press the Other Side for an answer as to what it is exactly that she is looking for, I am not given any further information. Third, Fay is gathering intelligence–that means just what it says at its face value–and that is the reason for her erratic pattern of movement and why she is here for such a long period of time.

As used to the bizarre and incredible as I am and in spite of the over 800 paranormal experiences I've had, and as used to the fantastic communications with the spirit world as I am, I have to admit: what the Other Side tells me about Fay floors me. It takes me awhile to try and wrap my mind around this information, and it bumfuzzles me for days.

Fay finally bids us adieu and I fire up my bike. I've got a major case of cabin fever. And for no particular reason I ride down to Titusville on I-95 south.

Coming up I-95 north is, to me, an astonishing sight: a convoy of a hundred or more electric company trucks! There could even be hundreds of trucks. There are trucks labeled with the name of an electric company in North Carolina, and there are some bearing the name of an electric company in Indiana. Folks have come from far, far away to help restore power to Florida after we've experienced Fay's fury, and I feel an immense sense of gratitude.

My ride brings with it another amazing sight: for a good portion of my ride the sides of both I-95 north and south are flooded; some trees are halfway under water. Fay flooded us, knocked out our power, and did who knows what other possibly supernatural things as well. And, whether intentionally or not, she also took the lives of 36 people.

I take it all in and I feel a sense of gratitude that we've come through as unscathed as we have, because in spite of all of the damage it could have been much, much worse: Fay could have decimated the entire state. She was a huge storm, and she hovered over Florida for days and eventually covered most, if not all, of the state with her girth.

I reach Titusville and I decide to shoot over to U.S. 1 north and ride back home that way, just for a change of scenery; a change of pace.

I'm happily tooling along at the speed limit, relaxed but keeping a wary eye on the sky...tornadoes form before, during, and after hurricanes (Fay has already gained notoriety for one of the most prolific tornado outbreaks on record), and I have just become visually aware of a towering thunderhead moving in from the east, but it appears to be several miles up the road which gives me plenty of time to think about what I want to do about it. If there's no lightning I can stop and put on my rain gear and ride on. I have ridden thousands of miles in everything from gentle showers to horrendous downpours; the rain doesn't bother me, but Florida is just about the lightning strike capital of the world so I must be careful, and I have to be correct in my assessment of this potential storm's danger; in fact my life may literally depend upon it.

So, I have a choice: I can keep riding up U.S. 1 for awhile longer, or I can head back west to I-95 north. The sky is clear to partly cloudy in that direction, and it looks as though I might be able to outrun the storm if I go that way.

While I'm riding along and trying to make up my mind about which way to go something very strange happens to the cloud formation of the giant thunderhead looming in front of me. And when I say very strange I *mean* very strange. I've watched the weather in Texas for years and I've seen some very odd things, but I've never seen anything quite like this: the thunderhead fans apart into two overlapping layers, remaining joined at its bottom, much like you'd fan a pair of cards open. That startling effect alone is enough to make me stare at this weird development, but what's really uncanny is that the top of one of the layers of the thunderhead, I swear to you, is in the shape of a perfect profile silhouette of the Disney character Goofy, and the top of the other layer shares the *exact same shape*. It's as if someone had put a giant mirror behind the foremost layer of cloud and now I'm seeing a perfect reflection of it...of Goofy. Well...I do live in Florida...

And then something even more incredible happens: the thunderhead opens up yet once again, fanning apart into two *additional* overlapping layers so that there are now four overlapping layers all joined at the bottom. Imagine fanning four cards apart so that they're all sharing a common pivot point at their bottoms and that they're wide enough that you can see each card's face but they all still overlap. The back two overlapping layers share the "Goofy" shape, and the front two overlapping layers are twins of each other too, and the shape they share at their tops reminds me of a crescent moon, or maybe Pac Man.

So there's a "bottom" layer that's a very dark cloud that looks like "Goofy," a cloud layer that's lighter in color overlapping that one that mirrors exactly the "Goofy" shape, still another layer overlapping that one that looks like a large crescent moon or "Pac Man" and is a shade of color somewhere between the dark and light of the other two, and finally the "top" layer which mirrors "Pac Man" exactly and is yet another shade of color.

This awesome, if not slightly ominous, cloud display has occurred in a matter of only a few minutes time and I've been so engrossed watching it (and trying to keep from crashing due to inattention to the traffic at the same time) that I haven't planned out how I need to continue my ride, but I'm thinking at this point that perhaps it's not a good idea to ride into the strange cloud. Maybe it's one of Fay's relatives and it might be looking for something, too...like maybe a biker to devour.

Out of respect I send the thought to the cloud that I appreciate the incredible (and bizarre) demonstration, and then I notice a sign at an intersection up ahead that shows I- 95 as a left turn there, and I'm in the far right lane. I have to make up my mind fast about what I'm going to do: am I going to continue to ride toward this incredibly bizarre and slightly ominous thunderhead which is performing weird artistic feats and seems to become more weird and dangerous-looking with each incarnation of itself, or shall I veer off and head back to I-95 and hope that I outrun the storm?

I check my left rearview mirror and take a quick glance over my left shoulder, and that's when I notice him: a fellow biker coming up on my left in the left lane. He overtakes me as I begin to slow down and continue to try to figure out what I should do, and he looks at me intently and smiles and gives a little nod or wave. I don't think there's anything unusual about that as we bikers are usually pretty friendly to one another but it's the particular *way* that he looks at me that strikes me as just a little bit odd.

He swerves over into the left turn lane to head toward I-95 and for some reason I feel compelled to follow him, so I check over my shoulder once again, find that traffic is clear, and I also head toward the left turn lane just as this other biker makes his turn onto the long, straight, flat road that heads toward a junction with I-95. I wait for traffic to clear so that I can turn, too, which only takes a few seconds time, and when I turn onto the long, straight, flat road I'm so gobsmacked that I nearly fall off my bike, for my fellow biker has completely disappeared, bike and all.

I shake my head in disbelief and I look for small side roads or parking lots or any place at all he could have turned off onto, and no such exit exists. And for him to make it so far up this long road that he would be completely out of sight in such a short few seconds time he would have had to have been riding a rocket, not a motorcycle. (Or maybe one of those light-speed UFOs...)

I gather my wits about me and ride to the junction of I-95 and head north, toward home. The weird thunderhead stays off to my east and slightly behind me as I ride, and I finish my trip with clear skies and not a drop of rain, much less having ridden into the maw of a supernatural cloud.

Was the disappearing biker a guardian angel sent to beckon me to follow him to a safer route, or was he just another of the peculiar manifestations that showed up at about the same time that Fay did?

I'm not sure, but I am grateful for the safe ride home.

And *you,* my friends: keep your eyes on the skies...

As if a sentient hurricane and a disappearing biker weren't enough, within a few days of this incident my wife and I were leaving in our car to run an errand and we noticed a warning light which had activated on our neighbor's outside electrical box. My wife was driving so she backed the car down the street and then pulled into their driveway and told me to stay put, that she'd run up to their house and make sure that they knew of the alarm.

While sitting in the car there were four or five distinct, loud raps which came from the right rear of our car, on the side where I was sitting. They were the sounds that a person makes when they loudly rap on your car's trunk or perhaps the side of the car near the wheel well in order to get your attention.

My first thought was that perhaps, while Marjorie talked to our neighbor's wife that he had somehow snuck out of his house and had circled around behind my car and rapped loudly in an effort to startle me.

There were only two problems with that theory, however: one was that I would have seen him as he came out of his house, even if he were approaching me from his side yard; and two...the second I heard the raps I snapped my head around and, seeing no one, I immediately exited my car and looked around it and up and down the street...and there was not a soul in sight.

Many such strange paranormal manifestations seemed to either accompany Fay, or to be precipitated or intensified by her.

And me...I have much more research to do concerning the possibility of intelligent storms. There are some disconcerting thoughts that occur to me. If a storm itself is intelligent, or directed by an intelligence or intelligences, then why the hideous destruction wreaked by floods, hurricanes, tornadoes, and hurricanes?

The heartbreaking loss of life and limb and property associated with these storms is monumental. I realize that Nature is not human hearted, but my god, the heartbreak and loss associated with these storms is awful to bear, a hardship incredibly difficult to endure. Why?

Is it because some of these controlling entities are tricksters? Maybe even malevolent in nature?

Or is it because someone or something is being punished for some sin or transgression, and those other human beings who have the misfortune to live around that individual who is being punished, those perhaps otherwise innocents whose lives and properties are destroyed, are they collateral damage in a war of which we know nothing about?

I wish I knew.

However I will share with you one thing that I've learned to do that has very powerful and positive effects. I have developed certain rituals that I follow to invoke safety and protection for me and my family, our home and property, and indeed, our city, whenever I become aware of the possibility of an approaching violent storm.

I attempt to communicate with the approaching intelligences and I ask them for their pity and their compassion.

And so far the Powers That Be have honored that, and we've been spared any serious destruction.

I wish I could tell you exactly what to do in the same circumstances, but I suspect that it's a path that you'll have to discover on your own.

But I'll tell you one thing: the spirits seem to be awfully fond of offerings of Gin...

CHAPTER

# Midnight in the Garden of Good and Evil

WHEN MY WIFE and I first became a couple we enjoyed many road trips together. During one of those trips we stayed at a hotel in San Antonio, Texas, ordered room service hamburgers, and watched on TV the movie, *Midnight in the Garden of Good and Evil*. Little did I realize at the time how significant this movie would be to me in years to come. Or rather, Bonaventure Cemetery…

I thoroughly enjoyed both the book and the movie, *Midnight in the Garden of Good and Evil,* and since I try to ride, purely for pleasure, to Savannah, Georgia and back a couple of times a year I have decided that on this upcoming trip I will make Bonaventure Cemetery my destination. I am taking along my digital camera, my film camera, and my digital voice recorder so that I can attempt to capture ghost photographs and EVP (Electronic Voice Phenomena). I had hoped that I might get Jim Williams' spirit voice greeting me with, "Hello, Sport!" but I'm disappointed to learn that he's not buried in Bonaventure but instead he is interred in the cemetery of his hometown.

It's a beautiful, sunny Florida day in April, 2009, but still a tad chilly on the bike as I ride north, but that's okay: I'm basking in the warmth of a leather jacket layered over a sweatshirt layered over a t-shirt. I decide to skirt I-95 north through Jacksonville by taking I-295 north instead and as I'm tooling along I look over and guess who I see? A pair of geese flying low to the ground as they pass by me headed in the opposite direction. It's as if they want to make sure that I see them.

Remember in my story *Funereal Aethereal* that I mentioned seeing the pair of geese at the Tallahassee Automobile Museum and intuitively understanding at the time that I should take them to be an omen. This morning I look and there they are again. Are they the same geese? Probably not, but I don't know for sure. All I know is that they once again seem to present themselves to me as an omen of some sort, and as a result I feel sure that Bonaventure Cemetery is going to provide me with some very interesting psychic experiences today.

After a pleasant and uneventful journey of 200-plus miles I am in Savannah, taking the streets that will lead me to Bonaventure Cemetery, and on one of these streets is a very large, colorful painted sign for a "psychic," and her lit neon sign in the window proclaims, "Open." I laugh aloud as I recall my experiences with some of these so-called "psychics." I'm not saying that this particular lady is a fraud; I'd have to personally investigate her in order to determine that, but I will say that I discover that among Savannah's "psychics" there is a Mrs. *Hope,* and a Mrs. *Grace,* and I begin to wonder if there's also a Mrs. Faith and a Mrs. Charity too. Lawsy, as the old folk say.

I finally arrive at the gates of Bonaventure Cemetery, which is listed in the National Register of Historic Places. Bonaventure can only be described as a beautiful, awe-inspiring, Gothic *dream* of a destination if you love cemeteries, and I do. I love to commune with whatever spirits happen to be there when I'm visiting; I love the ornate tombstones; and periodically I feel like it doesn't hurt to view cemeteries as giant works of art, huge forms of Memento Mori, not too subtle reminders to me that I am mortal too, and even though I now only grasp the fact abstractly (Don't we all think we will live forever, that we will somehow be the one to cheat Death?) nonetheless someday, after my spirit has departed from it, the physical remains of my body shall also reside in such a place; visiting a cemetery can be a very profound experience in more ways than one.

Actually my hope is to die at speed on my bike. Marjorie says that if I do to please make sure that my demise occurs at such high speed that there's a fiery crash and Melissa and I are consumed by the flames, relieving her of the necessity and expense of a funeral. Thanks Doll.

I park Melissa and unpack my gear, and after a brief chat with one of the cemetery's personnel I head to the office to pick up a map. Outside the office I discover a public restroom, a soda machine, a little area to sit and relax, and there are also numerous trashcans placed around the cemetery. This is obviously a popular tourist destination, and besides myself there are several other tourists here today too.

I'm not antisocial (Marjorie would beg to differ) but I try to get off away from the other folks so that I can be by myself...I want to focus fully on the paranormal realm, and I also want to try and obtain some EVP and I don't want any chattering voices from my fellow visitors around me when I do.

The psychic energy in the cemetery is warm and relaxing, and I have no doubt that Bonaventure holds a wealth of paranormal communication for me to experience in the future. Today, however, I'm rushed: I have to make it back home before day's end. I'm also over-awed by the plethora of large, exquisite, ornate tombstones, statues, monuments, and mausoleums. It's as enjoyable for me to behold them as it is for me to hunt ghosts.

But I finally wrest my attention away from the artsy side of this beautiful cemetery and I direct my focus back to business: hunting ghosts. I take out my Nikon film camera and shoot a roll of film. I take out my Kodak digital camera and shoot several photos. And then I begin my EVP recordings. I wander down toward the back of the cemetery which is bordered by the Wilmington River, and I stand a few moments and allow myself to enjoy the view. I turn around and the first thing I behold is a tiny grave that's only a few feet long, and my heart sinks.

I walk over to the tombstone and I calculate from the dates of birth and death that this young boy was only 1 year and seven months old when he died, and this fact pisses me off no end, because here I am, a grizzled old bastard no more deserving of life than anyone else, and I've been blessed to enjoy fifty-five years of it at the time I stand over this young child's grave, while this poor little soul never got to taste any of this old world's joys and pleasures. This hurts me.

All of my life I've lived close to dying and death and loss: I have literally held the hand of the dying as they have crossed over to the Other Side and I have felt their grips go limp as their spirits have left their bodies. I've preached funerals; I preached my own father's funeral, and *that* was hard! I have lived with the fact of death and dying all of my life, and because of my psychic gifts I've probably been more acutely aware of the great issues surrounding life and death than the person who isn't so gifted, and I have had to be the one to be stoic and calm in the face of such grievous loss and sorrow...I have had to be the one to comfort and console and guide those who have lost loved ones... and it would be logical to think that I am somehow numb to this whole death and dying thing by now but I'm not, and this little grave is the straw that finally breaks the camel's back and it's hard for me not to cry as I stand here.

One thing that I've learned over the years, both from my own personal experience and the experiences of others, is that losing a loved one to death *hurts,* and that hurt never goes away, not even with the passing of years.

So now, as I stand here looking at this tiny, tiny grave, I think of the family who more than likely rejoiced in the birth of their son, grew to love him, watched him begin to grow and then shared together their hopes and dreams for what his life would eventually become, and then they had all of that pulled away from them before their beloved child could even taste life. In less than two years' time he was yanked away from them. I mentally memorialize their tears and their mourning, and I am indignant that Death should throw such a tiny grave into our faces. It makes me mad! I feel the resentment building inside of me toward this inescapable fact of our life here on Earth: death. I say aloud, "Damn!" It's a curse meant for the Grim Reaper.

Yes, I believe in the Afterlife; I believe that our souls, spirits, whatever, live on; I believe that our intelligences, memories, and personalities survive the deaths of our physical bodies, but let me tell you something: in spite of my strong beliefs about the afterlife, death still angers me. Especially when the Reaper's dismal scythe falls on one so young and tender.

Have the young child's parents met up with him on the Other Side? I hope so; I believe so. But does that make up for the depth of painful emotions that they experienced for all those long years when they had to live without him? It seems to me like that hurt would last for a long, long time. And if you are reunited on the Other Side, wouldn't you worry that: "Well, we lost him once before. Is it possible that we can lose him yet again?"

I shake my head at such painful thoughts and I hold up my recorder. It's the final attempt I will make at recording a spirit voice before I have to leave if I'm going to make it home today. Softly I ask, "Is there anything anyone wants to say?" And then I press the record button and fall silent as I allow about ten seconds for a response from someone I can't see with my physical eyes, nor hear with my physical ears.

I blow a kiss to the tiny grave and I attempt to swallow my anger and to remain stoic in the face of this loss and grief; after all, bikers are supposed to be tough.

Back home the next day I upload my photos from my digital camera and, while I've captured much of Bonaventure's beauty, I haven't captured any paranormal phenomena; no ghosts.

I develop the roll of film; still no ghostly images.

I listen very carefully to each recording I made at the cemetery, one at a time, listening to each one over and over and over before moving on to the next. I've listened to nine recordings so far and I've not heard so much as a peep from the spirits.

And then, at the start of the tenth recording, the last one that I made as I stood before that tiny, tiny grave and asked if anyone had anything they wanted to say, I make out the words of a spirit's voice.

And those words ask me a question, and when I listen carefully to the recording and finally make the question out I get chills, because it becomes obvious to me that someone who I could not see with my physical eyes was standing there at that tiny grave with me, and it becomes obvious that that invisible person was reading my facial expressions, listening to my curse, possibly even reading my thoughts, for the ghost asks me:

"Are you angry?"

How does it make you feel to realize that invisible presences see us, watch us, hear us…listen to our words; maybe even read our very thoughts! Kind of a weird thing to think about, isn't it? I've heard people who have come to this realization proclaim that now they're a little self-conscious when it comes to getting naked and showering, or making love.

Kind of puts a whole new perspective on that old Bible verse, doesn't it?

"Therefore, since we are surrounded by such a great cloud of witnesses, let us throw off everything that hinders and the sin that so easily entangles."

CHAPTER **X**

# Life-saving Guidance

SO HERE I am, flying up I-75 north on my sweet Melissa.

It's a beautiful day with plenty of blue sky and sunshine. I'm feeling good, Melissa's running great, and it's only around noon; I still have half the day left to ride! Ah, down time: it feels so good. Time off for me to ride and play and relax.

I'm tooling along in the right lane (there are three lanes on I-75 north) and I'm going the speed limit of 70 miles per hour and I'm enjoying the scenery, and the feeling of motion, and I'm thinking no thoughts in particular and I'm not in any hurry to be anywhere and suddenly my feel good time is interrupted by a familiar voice in my head, and the voice says, very specifically, "Move into the far left lane."

Hmm…I don't *want* to move over into the far left lane: I'm comfortably situated in traffic with plenty of room to maneuver in my lane if something goes wrong, and after assessing traffic conditions I'll have to do some mighty tall riding to wiggle through this tightly packed speeding traffic to get into the left lane. I can handle the mighty tall riding easily, but I don't want to do it. I'm cruising along comfortably at the speed limit, and I don't *want* to ride faster; I want to take in the scenery and relax and not have to be as attentive as I will have to be at higher speeds.

Of course me obeying the speed limit means that little old ladies on tricycles are passing me in a blur. In Florida on the Interstates there are *three* speed limits, none of them the posted one of seventy miles an hour: in the right lane, which is traditionally the "slow" lane, you go 80 plus miles an hour; in the middle lane you go 90 plus; and in the left lane all bets are off. I'm not exaggerating. I think the left lane is the lane favored by those who imagine they are training to race the Daytona 500.

But only a few seconds later the voice speaks again, with a solemn insistence, and now calls me by name: "John; move into the far left lane."

I sigh. I know better than to continue to argue with the Powers That Be. I downshift, grab a handful of throttle, and throw my heavy iron beast to the left. I have to do some intricate up shifting/down-shifting/throttle on/throttle off/brakes on/brakes off /lean-and-weave skillful riding to get into the left lane, but I do so without incurring too much road rage from my fellow travelers. *Damn bikers!*

So now I'm zooming along in the left lane at a rate of speed that I'm comfortable with and is far below my high speed riding capability but I did not want to be riding this fast right now and I'm wondering, *what in the world was that all about?* I keep checking my rearview mirrors and looking around me at the traffic but all seems safe and sound and then, suddenly, *only a few short moments* from when the voice told me to move over, I'm rolling through a traffic accident *as it's happening!* As it's happening: *in the right lane, where I was just riding a few seconds ago.* Debris from the wreck, hubcaps and other detritus, is rolling and bouncing across the lanes of the highway and all around me. Cars are jamming on their brakes and swerving to take evasive action.

I glance over and I look into the wide and fearful eyes of a man– yes, in the middle of this high speed melodrama playing out in mere seconds we actually make meaningful eye contact–as he wrestles with the steering wheel of his car, which is spinning around *in the right lane* and is now facing in the wrong direction on the one way Interstate as the other speeding drivers begin to slam on their brakes and begin their own evasive maneuvers. Debris scatters across the roadway like shrapnel.

I slow down and check my mirrors and glance back over my shoulder to see if I need to stop and render assistance, but other cars are already doing so and I know that the Highway Patrol will be on the way soon so I ride on.

It's taken much longer for me to tell you about this frightening incident than it took, start to finish, for it to happen. From the time that the voice first told me to move over into the far left lane until I was rolling through the wreck as it happened only about fifteen to thirty seconds had elapsed. Not much of a heads up, eh? But I realize a few things: the heads up was enough; my life and limb were spared. And I also realize that the Powers That Be could have had me avoid this stretch of road entirely today, but then I wouldn't have had this dramatic example to present to you which illustrates that powerful unseen forces can guide our lives and protect us...if we will listen to them.

I sail through this tragic accident completely unaffected and I go on to enjoy my ride, but I *wouldn't have* if I hadn't listened to, and obeyed, the voice that told me to move into the far left lane, away from the right lane where I had been, in which the wreck occurred literally mere seconds later; instead I would have slammed headlong into the spinning car as the man lost control, and no telling how many times I would have been hit by the traffic around me.

Many times people wonder why tragic accidents happen to them, or to those that they love. "Where were our Guardian Angels then?" they lament.

Look...we die. No matter how long and how charmed a life we may lead at some point we're going to die. Maybe everyone does have "an appointed time."

I have learned a couple of key points about staying safe in this old world. First we have to *listen*. We have to listen to the voices of Spirit. We need to cultivate our perceptions until we can hear those voices with some reliability.

But foremost is that when we have heard the voices of Spirit speak then we must *obey*. It would not have done me a bit of good that day to have clearly heard the voices warning me of danger if I hadn't have obeyed and done what they told me to do. Instead I would be learning what the Other Side is really like; in person.

Lastly, please be sure that you give generous thanks to the Powers That Be when they pull your fat from the fire. I'm sure that in the Spirit Realm, as on Earth, that gratitude goes a long, long way.

# CHAPTER XI

# Speaking of Dying at Speed on Two Wheels

SPEAKING OF DYING at speed on two wheels...this is what it feels like; *almost.*

Bikers–motorcyclists–*LOVE* their machines. There have been occasions when a woman in a relationship with a biker has given him an ultimatum: Me, or the bike! Most of the time the biker will choose the bike. This has nothing to do with the biker being a total jerk: he simply figures that he picked the wrong woman to begin with and he will choose more carefully in the future. That's how important the lifestyle is to us.

I acquired my first bike around the age of 15 or 16 and I've ridden ever since. Motorcycling is one of those things that can pretty much be counted on to fall in one of two ways: a person rides another biker's machine, or buys one of their own and learns to ride, and fears it horribly. This type of person is afraid of motorcycles: afraid of falling, either at speed or while standing still; afraid that they will not be able to control or properly maneuver their machine; afraid of road debris; afraid that an animal will bolt out of the woods and run into them; afraid of a wreck with a car or another motorcycle; afraid of the feelings of speed and raw power that the bike emanates. They will never be truly comfortable and happy on their machines, no matter how much they ride. If this is you… then motorcycling isn't for you; give the machine up. Sell it, and find another lifestyle, sport, or hobby with which to engage yourself.

And then there is the second type of person, such as myself: that very first ride is like a hit of the most pleasurable drug ever manufactured and there's an instant addiction to the pleasurable feelings of biking. It never goes away. A person craves more and more and more. It becomes a lifestyle around which everything else revolves.

I can no more imagine myself being without a motorcycle for the rest of my life than I can imagine being without my five physical senses and my psychic senses.

There have been god-awful portions of my lifetime when I have not owned a motorcycle for a period of time, mostly due to health reasons: if you face a long stretch of time when it's physically impossible to ride, it doesn't make much sense to have a beautiful machine sitting there wasting away. But that never kept me from thinking about bikes, wanting another one, remembering rides and experiences, and craving more.

I sometimes tell those who are just getting started in motorcycling that, if you do it right, it's almost as good as sex. Yes, it's that pleasurable for me.

Since most hardcore bikers feel the same way that I do about the lifestyle, most of us also share a credo: our preferred way to depart this old world would be to die while riding our machines at high speed, such as traveling down the Interstates. Understand…we don't want to take anyone else out with us, and we don't have a death wish: we have absolutely no desire to die before our times, because, god forbid, that would subtract pleasurable years from our motorcycling experience!

No, our end of life scenario goes roughly like this: We're up in years, and we know that the Reaper will be hunting us down before long. Rather than face long painful years at the hands of some dreadful and debilitating disease, or rather than waste away in some god forsaken retirement home, let us instead be traveling on one last long motorcycle trip, enjoying the scenery, fondly reminiscing about the good years of our lives, and then BAM!...fatal heart attack while we're traveling seventy miles an hour on a lonely back road, or in the wee morning hours on the Interstate when there's less traffic and our sudden and unexpected demise, replete with fiery crash and burn, won't cause anyone else any harm.

That's the way to go! John Russell of Florida died suddenly and unexpectedly while motorcycling from Florida to New York. He was 85 years old. Apparently Mr. Russell's brain exploded from multiple aneurisms and he lost control of his motorcycle while traveling at about 75 miles per hour on I-95 north. While no one else was injured Mr. Russell's crash was spectacular and fiery. Witnesses said that they had never seen a man remain attached to a motorcycle while it flipped and rotated and skidded so many times and for such a great distance. They further stated that when the bike, with Mr. Russell still apparently holding onto the handlebars in some type of bizarre death grip, finally came to a halt that the motorcycle exploded and burst into such dramatic flames that both the bike and Mr. Russell were virtually incinerated before anyone could put the fire out. He is survived by...

Moo ha ha. Insert smiley face emoticon here. Yep...that's the way I want to go. And I thought, for a moment, that I was about to get my wish one day.

I have told this story many times and I have yet to find another biker who has shared a similar experience.

Having survived the trauma it has become one of the absolute best stories that any biker could ever want to share. Yes, it's that good. But I would not want to experience it again, ever, unless it happened to coincide with my desire to depart this old Earth at speed on two wheels when I'm 85 years old. Or older.

I'm on I-95 south, heading home from one of my long pleasure rides. I have a few favorite rest stops that I frequent and I pull into one now to stretch my legs and to grab a snack and to get something to drink. A storm has been following me, moving north to south with me, but it's still some ways off in the distance. I feel sure that I will outrun it and that I will have plenty of time to make it home before it catches me, so I don't have any worries about stopping for a rest break.

As I'm standing there with my snack and my soda, watching the skies, I notice that a portion of the storm has moved a little more quickly than I anticipated and that it has begun to snake its way around to the west/southwest and then a portion of it has begun to curve eastward, toward me. The main body of the storm is still well north of my location, and this segment that has managed to catch up with, and now move past me, doesn't worry me too much as it doesn't show any signs of heavy rain or lightning, although it looks like it could develop into something if it wanted to. But for now the sun is still shining and nothing looks that threatening. The wind is picking up a little bit, but I have ridden against winds that were so strong that holding onto the handlebars was like holding half a chin-up for an hour to keep from being blown off the bike, so I ain't worried about the wind either.

I take my time finishing my snack and my soda and then I mount up and continue my ride.

As I come off of the on ramp and get back onto I-95 I am hit with a sudden blast of wind that threatens to rip me off of my bike and rocks me and my bike severely, almost blowing us over into the next lane. Damn. On the unofficial race course that is I-95 in Florida traffic is actually beginning to slow down: big trucks and even cars are having difficulty maintaining control in the wind. I'm thankful that they're slowing down, because for the first time in my lifetime of riding motorcycles the wind is of such high velocity that I'm feeling a little uneasy and I'm thankful for the opportunity to go a little more slowly. I'm keeping pace with the rest of the traffic as we battle to maintain control of our vehicles and to stay in our lanes; I glance down at my speedometer and we're only going about 50, maybe 55 miles an hour in a 70 mile per hour zone where traffic normally races along well above 80 or 90. This wind is a big deal to get drivers to slow down this much.

And then it happens. Again, it will take me much longer to tell you about it than it does to experience it, but while it is happening to me it feels like I am enduring a lifetime of fright and uncertainty before it's finally over.

The combined weight of me and my fully loaded bike is close to half a ton. Remember that. While I'm riding along with the rest of traffic and trying to maintain control against the increasingly powerful and unpredictable winds I look up the road and I see a familiar sight: the tall grasses and weeds and the shorter trees are bent over sideways, in places almost flat against the ground, and rippling violently as the wind rushes over them and pushes them over. I know what this means, because I grew up in West Texas and we lived in the southern tip end of Tornado Alley. This violent wind activity means that a tornado is either close by on the ground, or that a funnel cloud is dropping down and will probably become a tornado on the ground.

There's a small break in the trees that line the shoulder of the highway, a brief clearing that allows me to look out a ways into the landscape toward the west, the direction from which the wind is roaring. I scan the countryside but I don't see anything on the ground. The sun is still shining.

And right then it happens. As I'm riding along me and Melissa, my precious motorcycle, are picked up together, as one unit, into the air! I am not sucked off of her by this mischievous vortex; there isn't any space between my butt and the saddle. We are lifted up together as if a giant invisible hand has reached down and grabbed us, scooping us up from underneath, completely enclosing us in its fist and raising us up into the air. I can't tell you how many thoughts run so very quickly through my head, but the predominant one is, "Holy fucking shit! This cannot be happening!"

Now I don't mean that we are picked up three feet or 10 feet into the air; nothing that dramatic. But we are picked up a good six inches, maybe a foot, into the air; plenty enough drama. And...we begin to rotate slightly in a counterclockwise direction. That's what is scaring me the most about this surreal experience, because we're still moving forward at about 50 or 55 miles per hour through the air and I realize that if this wind sets me down sideways I will be completely, helplessly out of control. I will slam violently over sideways onto the asphalt at 55 miles per hour and then I will be run over by five or ten cars before people finally figure out what has happened and get stopped.

And then one final thought runs through my head: Well, I always said I wanted to go out at speed on two wheels. It looks like this is it. It looks like this is my day. My time has come. I wonder what the Other Side's going to be like? And who's going to take care of Marjorie?

And then this playful wind spins me and Melissa back clockwise but we're still at a slight angle to the roadway and I realize that even if the wind sets us down now I will still have to perform some fancy body english to keep from dumping the bike.

And the wind does...sit us down at that exact same, slightly out of kilter angle, and I say a quick prayer and I call upon all of the years and miles of motorcycling experience I have and I also count on some quick emergency help from the Other Side and I keep the bike upright, manage to correct for our angle of travel, get straightened out, and now I breathe a big sigh of relief for we're traveling in a straight line again with both wheels firmly on the pavement. Wow! Fleetingly a thought races through my head: what a great story this is going to make.

I glance up at the sky and there is a funnel cloud lowering straight toward me!

*Damn the winds.* I am suddenly fearless in the face of these dangerous winds. I lay down over my gas tank and I downshift and open my throttle all the way, winding the engine up until it screams before I upshift and open the throttle all the way again. I ain't hangin' around to see what else this tornado has in mind for me today! I don't know how fast I'm running to outrun this twister that wants to play with me, and I don't care. If there was a state trooper right beside me he'd have to wait for me to stop until I felt like I was finally free and clear of danger. I run hot until I'm about five miles or so down the road, and then I finally ease off of the throttle, sit up, glance over my shoulders and check my rearview mirrors. I don't see any tornado chasing me, so I begin to breathe a little easier and I say a lot of thanks to the Powers That Be.

The sun is still shining, I seem to have outrun the worst of the winds, no rain is falling, there's no lightning...I think I'm off scot-free. Whew; I breathe a big sigh of relief and I give more thanks to Those Who have pulled my fat from the fire.

A recent rule in my life is that I don't imbibe when I'm riding my bike, but I'm shook up enough by today's experience that I'm going to allow myself one bottle of beer when I get to my destination: a bar that has, in the same building, a tattoo parlor. Genius, I think; pure genius.

The head tattoo artist is running a promotional special in the hopes that it will attract more tattoo business: anyone can get a tattoo of the number 13 in honor of Friday the thirteenth, for thirteen dollars. Today is Thursday the twelfth but she runs the special for a few days on either side of the actual date. Since Friday the thirteenth is traditionally a lucky day for me and I associate good fortune with the number thirteen I am going to stop and get my tattoo.

I pull into the bar, order my bottle of beer, and I realize that I have become *him:* the grungy, grizzled old biker who has become invisible to pretty young women and has way too many bothersome stories to tell. Nevertheless I buttonhole anyone who will listen so that I can regale them with the story of the nearly life ending experience I've just now survived.

People listen respectfully, nodding, but looking at me with an expression that indicates that they think that I'm on something far more powerful than alcohol. After a few attempts at impressing the locals with my mind-boggling experience, I give up and stroll outside with my beer.

I spot the tattoo artist opening up shop and I go in to get my lucky number 13 tattoo, and while I'm regaling her with my story I look out the window. "Sumbitch, look at that," I tell her, and she glances out the window and together we watch this funnel cloud come snaking down out of the sky and it begins to elongate and undulate through the air like some kind of snake as it moves almost straight for the tattoo parlor...and me again! I thought I had gotten off scot-free.

"Looks like it followed you," she says calmly, not nearly as shaken up as I have suddenly become. We move to the window to watch it blow on over without incident. I shake my head in amazement and sit back down in the chair and she finishes my tattoo.

Well, with that experience I got an inkling of what it would be like to realize that I'm going out of this old world at speed on two wheels. I wouldn't have relished the pain of the crash and subsequently being run over no telling how many times before I expired, but surely it would beat lying in a hospital bed for months on end, in horrible pain, waiting for my last breath.

And because of this surreal experience that I have survived, here again is yet another storm cloud that interacts with me; but this one interacts with me in the most intimate way I've yet experienced.

The first cloud down in the parking lot by my car seemed to want to play tag, but kept its distance. The second cloud, the one that I encountered during the weird days of Fay, seemed to want to show me the cloud version of a shadow puppet show. This funnel cloud though seemed to want to get as up close and personal with me as possible, actually utilizing its winds to handle me, to get ahold of me and to feel me and my machine, to lift us up into the air, turning us around as if examining us, and then to follow me and watch while I got my tattoo. I'm beginning to put a lot of stock into the belief that storms are intelligent, or that they are at least directed by intelligent beings. Maybe not every storm, but...

It's an incredible feeling to fancy yourself this tough, strong, fearless biker roaring down the highways and to realize that there are forces that can specifically target you, pick you up into the air, have their way with you, and sit you down just enough off kilter that you get the message: "Hey, I could have really fucked you up or even killed you just now if I had wanted to!"

And then to have that same force follow you to your destination just to show you that they know who you are, where you were going, and that you can't outrun them or hide from them.

There's a lot of talk about respect in the biker world. It's one of the most important issues that there is among bikers. And I think that we, all of us who seek a deeper spiritual walk, have lost that healthy respect for the Other Side, for Ghosts, Angels, and the Spirits of the Dead who may know more than we do, have stronger powers than we do, and may possess vastly greater intelligence as well.

The Bible, the Christian Holy Book to which most people proclaim allegiance but don't have any vague idea of its contents, most of which they would find repulsive (God orders so many genocidal wars in the Old Testament that it's a wonder that anyone's left alive today!) and to which they act in contradiction to its guidance, has some interesting light to shed: "The fear of the Lord is the beginning of wisdom..."

Most theologians agree that the concept of fearing the Lord can best be understood if "fear" is instead translated as "reverential awe." Respect. Respect for a power that can lift you and your machine into the air, turn you to and fro as if inspecting a bit of produce for blight or damage, and then setting you back down in such a way that you know that you've encountered something much greater and more powerful than you will ever be.

How many so-called paranormal investigators blunder onto the scene and immediately begin to insult, challenge, and even curse the spirits that are there, challenging them to a fight...these fools are too arrogant to realize that if the Powers That Be chose to they could pick *them* up into the air, turning them to and fro while examining them, before perhaps choosing to drop them out of a second story window.

How many of our prominent televangelists have raised millions of dollars and procured lavish lifestyles for themselves, all the while disrespecting the Powers That Be by living in direct contradiction to what they so earnestly, and tearfully, preach.

How many phony psychics rob their clients of money and peace of mind, sowing fear and confusion in their wake, disrespecting a field that is already in severe disrepute to begin with and sneering at our common humanity in the process.

How many blithering idiots proclaim to have a handle on God, or to know *exactly* what the Other Side is like, or will tell you, for a fee, exactly how to obtain everything you want in life through manipulating the Powers That Be.

Mike Tyson...in my opinion one of the most fierce and greatest boxers of all time. You damn sure wouldn't go to his home, knock loudly on his door, and greet him when he answered with a barrage of threats, curses, and demands...would you? No.

Then why are you so damn arrogant as to believe that you can control and manipulate this incredible Power that could flick you away like a gnat if it chose to do so. It makes me think that there are more checks and balances in our interactions with the Spiritual Realm than we may realize.

Respect...it's not just in the biker world that this should be a topic of concern.

And my lucky number 13 tattoo? Well...I haven't been picked up into the air anymore since I got it...yet.

# Vic

WHEN WE MOVED to Florida I met a group of bikers with whom I occasionally rode. One of our crew was a bantam of a fellow named Vic.

Vic was tough as nails, ironically very sensitive (as many hardened bikers are), had a great sense of humor, and he was an absolute ace mechanic, especially when it came to motorcycles. I never saw him stumped by any mechanical or electrical problem and there seemed to be nothing that his muscular, oversized hands couldn't fix; except for Vic himself.

Vic had been seriously ill for a number of years and at the ridiculously young age of 46 he passed away. It really jars you when someone a decade younger than you are buys the farm.

His wife laid him out in state, at their church, in his leathers, including his leather vest which was embellished with a plethora of pins that commemorated various motorcycle rallies and events and also bore various emblems, symbols, and sayings. Vic loved those pins. He was really proud of the pin collection he displayed on his leather vest.

In his open casket along with some assorted motorcycle memorabilia was a very symbolic and meaningful wrench inserted into his large, capable, folded hands.

On a stand nearby was Vic's leather jacket.

We came to the church to pay our respects, many of us on our bikes even though it was frigid weather, dressed in our jeans, leather vests, and leather jackets. It was the only fitting and proper way to show up.

Vic's funeral service was to be followed by his cremation and the outline of the service was that we, his old riding buddies, would show up in full gear on our motorcycles and after the service we would ride escort behind the hearse as it drove Vic to the crematorium, after which we would all break off for a short memorial ride.

It was a beautiful, sunny, clear day; but *cold.* I had on thermal gear with three additional layers and I was miserable. About twenty plus other bikers braved the cold to ride in honor of Vic's memory, and we parked together in the church parking lot and grouped together to talk before we went inside for the service.

I hate funeral services...I'm an ordained minister and I've preached them. I preached my own father's funeral service, at his request, and man–was that ever hard. I believe firmly in the Afterlife, but that still doesn't ease the pain and heartache of losing a loved one. Death is a rough business.

Finally it was time and we all went inside the church, all of us in our jeans and boots and leathers, and we sat together as a group. Man...you've never seen so many tough bikers, myself included, trying so hard to choke back tears.

When the service was over we gathered together in the parking lot for one last ride with our dear departed friend. The order of the procession was, first: a police motorcycle escort; second: the hearse carrying Vic's body to the crematorium; third: the two-abreast pack of bikers following the hearse as rear escorts.

At his widow's request when we mounted our bikes and started our engines we all began to rev our engines repeatedly, filling the tranquil morning air with the multiple loud roars of motorcycle exhausts. It was both a salute and an acknowledgement that Vic would be riding with us, if only in spirit, and that we, by god, were still one step ahead of the Reaper. Many cultures fling noise in the face of Death: "Hey, by god, we're still alive, sumbitch! You didn't get us yet!" It's a false bravado, I fear; we know that the Reaper's scythe will fall on us too, but it's a way to convince ourselves that *not today.*

We are choking back tears as we line up behind the hearse carrying Vic. Revving our engines and blasting our protest at the Grim Reaper with all of the noise that we can muster helps us to strengthen our resolves not to cry.

More police block traffic, the police motorcycle escort begins to move, and then the hearse, and then we bikers, formal, solemn, two-abreast, revving our engines as loudly as possible as we exit the church parking lot and file onto the street.

My wife, who has come to the funeral in our car and is standing with Vic's wife, watching from the parking lot, tells me later that Vic's widow held his leather jacket high in the air with both hands as the funeral procession rode away from the church, a scenario that I'm glad I did not witness: I would have teared up so badly it would have been impossible to continue to ride.

We follow the hearse until it turns off to deliver Vic's body to the crematorium.

As we peel off to conduct our memorial ride we again rev our engines loudly, honk our horns, and give Vic little salutes as the hearse turns one way and we turn another.

In one direction a hearse delivers a friend's body to be consumed by flames.

In the other direction his friends ride; still alive in their bodies.

Being psychic I took special notice of a very odd fact during the memorial ride. When riding as a group it is inevitable, even on a very short ride, that some riders will not make a red light and will fall behind the pack. The pack will notice, pull over and wait, and resume the ride when the other riders catch up. It's not uncommon to have this happen several times during a group ride, but today, on our memorial ride of approximately 18-20 miles or so, no one, not a single rider, gets caught by a red light. Either the entire pack makes the green light and stays together, or the lead riders get caught by the red light and so the entire pack is stopped together. This never happens. The other bikers notice it too.

My first thought is that Vic is somehow orchestrating this uncommon experience from the Other Side so that we know that he not only has seen our memorial ride for him but that he is actually participating in it!

This eventually proves to not be just sentimental conjecture on my, or anyone else's part, but the first in a long and powerful series of communications from Vic.

My wife and I have purchased new cell phones, but we have kept the old ones. I'm not sure why; spares? Backups? Eventual gifts to some charity that will utilize them somehow? Anyway, the old phones still have their batteries; they still turn on and off; they are just not functional: our service has been transferred to our new phones, and the old phones cannot make or receive calls or text messages.

I have turned my old phone off and put it away.

For some bizarre reason my wife has left her old phone on, instead of turning it off and putting it away. And she has set it on a glass-topped side table that stands on her side of our couch.

One night not long after Vic's funeral service we are sitting at our dining table. We've just finished dinner and we're sitting there talking before we rise and clean up the dinner dishes, and the conversation turns to Vic, and *as* we're reminiscing about him we both begin to hear a loud, odd, intermittent buzzing noise. I remember looking at Marjorie and saying aloud, "What the hell?!"

When we finally pinpoint the direction of the noise we realize that it's coming from our living room, and its cause is her old cell phone: it is set to "vibrate" when receiving an incoming text message or phone call and now it is vibrating and as it vibrates it does a buzzing noisy dance all over that glass table top. I pick up the phone and it continues to vibrate as if receiving an incoming text message or an incoming phone call. There's just one problem: that is a literal physical impossibility, for the service to this phone is disconnected!

The vibration finally stops. Although I know that it's impossible for this phone to receive a call, a voice mail, or a text message I check anyway, but there is no incoming call or text message shown.

Marjorie and I both look at each other and we say it simultaneously: "Vic!"

In the weeks and months to come I find out that Vic has repeatedly called other phones from his cell phone, his number showing up as an incoming call. One person that Vic had left a voice message with keeps receiving an incoming call from Vic on his phone, and when he checks it there is that old voice message, again and again, with each new incoming call. And Vic's wife receives some of the most incredible and irrefutable signs that Vic is watching over her and communicating with her.

A riding buddy from our group, which included Vic, asks me to take a ride with him.

Most bikers wear leather vests, and these vests are decorated with patches and pins commemorating motorcycling events, the passing of friends, political statements, and various symbols associated with the motorcycling lifestyle.

Vic's vest was a plethora of pins and patches; I got frustrated with wearing a vest covered with pins because at speed, even when my vest was snapped shut, the fluttering of the vest would somehow manage to loosen the backs of the pins and they would fly off with the result that I would lose not only the back that held the pin on but the pin itself as it was blown off of my vest by the wind or fell off due to the vibrations my body experiences from the bike. Not every rider experiences that frustration but I did, regularly enough that I stopped wearing a vest with pins on it. It became frustrating to spend five dollars or more on a really nice pin only to have the back come off of it with the result that the pin fell off of my vest somewhere out on the highway never to be seen again.

I once asked Vic how come none of his pins ever blew off as we raced down the road at high speed.

"I superglue the backs on," he told me with his trademark grin.

Pins were a big deal with Vic, kind of another one of his trademarks.

And my riding buddy today has a vest similarly covered with pins. And oddly enough even when his vest is open and flapping wildly in the wind, as it is today, he never seems to have a pin come off. Not ever.

So today after our ride we wind up at a watering hole that we all regularly rode to, especially when Vic was still alive and rode with us. This place has significance for us, and had significance for Vic as well.

We park our bikes, dismount, and lean against our machines as we chat a bit in the parking lot before going inside. Of course the talk turns to Vic, and as it does the pins on my friend's leather vest begin to fly off like popcorn escaping a pan!

But the pins don't just begin to fly off of the front of his vest...the *backs* of the pins begin to fly out *from inside of his vest,* shooting out at odd angles and at amazing speed. The pins, and the backs, travel through the air three feet, five feet, even ten feet before landing on the ground.

"What the hell?" my friend curses.

As he bends down to begin to pick up his pins and their backs more of the pins and backs suddenly begin to fly off of the front of his vest and from inside of his vest.

He looks up at me, bumfuzzled. "What in the hell is going on?" he asks me, and I'm grinning like a possum that's eating briars and I answer him with one word that explains it all: "Vic."

He shakes his head as he continues to pick up pins and backs, pinning them back into place on his vest. "It must be," he says.

I remind him how big a deal Vic's pins were to him, and how much he loved that vest of his that was covered with pins.

"Vic's here," I tell him. "He's letting us know that he's with us."

My friend agrees. It's the only thing that makes sense, the only thing that can rationally explain this odd phenomenon. Finally the pins and backs quit popping like some kind of bizarre popcorn and we go and grab a couple of libations with which to toast our old buddy. It's a beautiful day so we decide to sit outside in the sunshine. As we talk my buddy tells me about a phone experience he has had with Vic.

He got up one morning after Vic's funeral and in his incoming calls there was one from Vic's cell phone! He called Vic's widow and asked her where Vic's cell phone was. She told him that it was sitting on their fireplace mantle in their home, where it had been since Vic died.

"Well, I don't appreciate what you've done. I don't find it funny, not one bit. I think it's a pretty crappy practical joke to play on someone, especially this close to Vic's funeral."

Taken aback she asked him what in the world he was talking about and he says that he doesn't think that it's funny that she got Vic's cell phone and called him with it.

She explains to him that Vic's phone has sat there on the mantle, along with some other artifacts of his, turned off and untouched since his funeral.

As my buddy is telling me this story the pins suddenly start flying off of the front of his vest again, as well as the backs flying out of the inside of his vest, once again shooting out at odd, impossible angles and for great distances.

"It's Vic again, confirming that he's with us and showing us that he is indeed the one communicating with us by producing this phenomenon with your vest!" I tell him. He is dumbfounded. I'm impressed.

The pins and backs once again finally quit flying off, we toast our dear old buddy, fire up our bikes, and head home.

But this turns out to be only one in an ongoing series of communications from Vic, communications that have lasted for months and now, for years.

I didn't know Vic that long, and so I don't know how good a buddy he considered me to be, but when my time comes to cash in my chips I hope a couple of things turn out to be true: one, that there are motorcycles on the Other Side; and two, that Vic is there to greet me as I cross over and that we share my first ride there, together.

I have ridden solo to a bike night event at this same watering hole.

I'm sitting watching the bikes come and go, and my thoughts turn to Vic. He had this old Harley he had customized himself, he being an ace mechanic, welder, fabricator, and more. And the odd thing that none of us could ever figure out was the strange noises that emanated from Vic's bike if you were riding behind him.

Bizarre and odd whistles and wheezes and ringings and tinklings...all emanating from a bike that we knew to be mechanically sound because Vic would not let it be otherwise. This hopped up bike of his would even give sport bikes a serious run for their money it was such a hot rod and ran so well.

I'm thinking about that and a short, wiry fellow with a build very close to Vic's pulls into the parking lot, on a brand spanking new custom chopper. As he parks he makes eye contact with me, and we nod. I almost get chills: he looks like Vic, but he doesn't. He gets off of his bike, walks into the watering hole, and I almost get up to follow, but in just a minute or two he comes back out and gets on his bike, fires it up, and begins to ride away, very slowly, and from the rear of his machine comes those same bizarre sounds that used to come from Vic's bike. I've been a biker since I was about 15, and I've been around bikes my whole life, and I have never heard any other bike but Vic's emanate such strange noises, and I can't help but wonder...

Why? Why do some folks seem to be able to communicate with us from the Other Side so powerfully, meaningfully, and effectively; and yet most people left behind that also yearn for some sign from a loved one go throughout their lives without even the most simple sign to bring them comfort.

I don't know. I don't think anyone does. It's been a topic of interest and frustration for as long as anyone can remember.

Why are some communications so dramatic, and yet others so banal? Why was I singled out to have experienced almost 900 of them so far, and yet there are other psychics, both real and so-called, that rarely if ever experience any paranormal phenomena.

I think some of it has to do with persistence: if you refuse to give up trying to receive some type of meaningful communication from a loved one I believe that you will increase your chances of receiving that communication.

But, when it comes, for god's sake *please* don't discount it or, even worse, write it off as coincidence.

Take it for the treasured gift that it is, respect it, honor it, cherish it, and be glad that we have this evidence that life goes on, that there is something above and beyond what we see with our eyes in this old world every day, and that we have a hope of, if not a glorious reward and ease from pain and strife, at least a chance to understand and continue to grow.

What's it all about? Is there really a Heaven and a Hell? Which religion is right? Which belief system works?

There are no reliable answers, in spite of what others would try to cajole you into believing.

No one really knows, and it's been that way ever since mankind has tried to understand this greater and more powerful spiritual realm which confronts us, teases us, pulls at us, entices us, and sometimes, just sometimes...grants our desires, or pulls the curtain back just enough to give us a little peek at the truth, a little glimpse of how things might be, another small piece of the puzzle.

And the truth of it all? Well, to quote from a movie: "You can't handle the Truth!"

And maybe we can't. Maybe we aren't supposed to understand, or maybe it's that we *can't* understand.

One of my favorite scenes in one of my favorite movies, *The Mothman Prophecies,* has the protagonist asking a paranormal researcher that, if these intelligences are so much smarter than we are why don't they just reveal themselves to us and explain themselves to us?

The researcher replies that well, you're smarter than a cockroach...have you ever tried explaining yourself to one?

# Catch a Falling Star

I EXPLAINED TO you that I have had these amazing paranormal experiences since I was a kid, long before I began a motorcycling way of life. You certainly don't have to own a motorcycle to have psychic or paranormal experiences; it just makes it a heck of a lot more fun when you do. Actually I guess I *have* been a biker since I was a kid: I started riding a bicycle at an early age and from my succession of bicycles I grew to have a love affair with anything on two wheels. Another thing that I tell people who are contemplating buying their first motorcycle is that if you rode, and *loved,* bicycles as a kid then more than likely you will love motorcycling too.

Anyway, of all of the exciting supernatural things I heard and saw as a young boy the one that impressed me the most and that still remains vivid in my mind to this day is when my mother and I saw a falling star; a big, five-pointed, glowing, yellow-colored falling star. Up close and personal.

Of course we all know that stars are *round* objects; our sun, for example, which is round, is a massive star, and so far, as far as I know, the Hubble Space Telescope has failed to detect anything pentagram-shaped in space. Certainly it has never detected anything with the shape that we drew as kids to portray twinkling stars in the nighttime skies of our crayon drawings.

But that classic pentagram-shaped star is *exactly* the shape of the object that fell from the skies into a vacant lot beside our friend's home…

Ha! You think that because I'm only around 10 or 12 years old that I *can't* be a biker yet, but I am: I have terrorized my neighborhood no end on my Schwinn Stingray. Once I attached so many playing cards to my fender with clothespins so that they would impact the wheel's spokes and make a "motor" noise that I couldn't hear a real motorcycle riding by me the other way down the street. Yeah, our neighbors call my mom periodically to complain about all the noise that I make. I guess I was trying to scare off the evil spirits even way back then.

Anyway, it's summertime in West Texas (think sticking your head inside of a pizza oven and trying to breathe) and the car my mom owns, a '52 Chevy, doesn't have air conditioning so we always leave the windows down in hot weather during the day because we don't want to come outside and get into a blast furnace on four wheels, and of course leaving all of the car's windows down makes locking any of the car's doors pointless; we roll up the windows and lock the car's doors at night, when we're done using it for the day.

Today we're going to visit some friends of ours who live in the north part of town, and for some reason my mother pulls in front of their house and parks facing the "wrong" way, that is, into oncoming traffic. What I don't know now is that far into the future such a maneuver will merit you a ticket, but today it either isn't much of an issue, or else the police are just looking the other way.

We park in front of our friend's house, facing east. Their house sits on a corner lot, facing south, and directly east across the street from their house is a vacant lot, one of many we have in San Angelo back then, and the lot is filled with mesquite trees, scrub brush, cactuses, and various grasses and weeds, which are all bone dry in the heat of our blistering West Texas summer.

With it being summertime and a real scorcher when we arrive (at about 3 in the afternoon) we leave our car's windows down, and the car's doors, naturally, unlocked.

After a pleasant but uneventful visit which lasts several hours we finally bid our friends farewell just as it's reaching one of the darkest stages of twilight outside. Mom will definitely need to turn on the car's headlights in order to see to drive.

We say our goodbyes to our friends while standing on their front porch, and they watch us walk down their sidewalk and get into our car. They wave a final goodbye before shutting their front door.

And it's then that I see it!

Mom has started the car's engine when, falling very slowly, almost in slow motion, a perfectly symmetrical five-pointed star–yes, a pentagram–falls from the sky in a gentle arc right in front of us, and its trajectory is carrying it into that bone dry vacant lot next to our friend's house.

"Mom! Look!" I shout, somewhat unnecessarily of course, for my mother is transfixed; her eyes are locked onto the object as it falls.

It has a pretty, yellow phosphorescent or luminescent glow as if lit from within, and it trails a short tail behind it like a comet might; the tail dissolves as the star falls. The star is as large as the side of a house, and seems to be no more than several inches to a foot thick, and it's a flat object rather than being rounded or bulbous.

What's so bizarre is how *slowly* it falls! It's a striking, beautiful sight, but it terrifies my mother who begins to literally shout for me to lock all the car doors, and to roll up the windows. My first thought is that we don't *have* to worry about this paranormal phenomenon because we're going to suffocate in the car from the heat. My mother, who has lived her life exuding a false bravado, is frightened, more frightened than I have ever seen her be before.

Me, on the other hand, I want to get out and go investigate. (I don't know if I've always had an uncommon bravery, or an uncommon stupidity.)

I ask my mother about exiting the car in order to get an even closer look at the mysterious object but she absolutely forbids it. She puts the car into gear and starts to drive off, but I stop her with a query: "Mom, it's bone dry in that field, in that vacant lot." The vacant lot covered a good half block, maybe more. "If that star falls in there, won't it set it on fire? And won't our friends be in danger? And shouldn't we wait to see what happens so if the star does cause a fire we can run back up to our friend's house and use their phone to call the fire department?"

My mother reluctantly agrees that there is indeed some merit to my suggestion, although complying necessitates that we remain in proximity to this unknown and, to her, extremely frightening object.

We watch, both of us transfixed, as the star slowly falls into the midst of the vacant lot, falling down among the trees into the dry grasses and weeds, trailing its tail as it goes.

The star gives off such a bright glow that we can see its light shining through the trees. We continue to watch, and the star's glow begins to dim, more and more until, gradually, the glow winks out completely and darkness resumes control of the night.

There is no fire, no aftermath of any kind that we can notice, and my mother drives home much faster than usual tonight as I pepper her with questions that she can never answer.

After we're miles away from our friend's house and the mystifying star she finally allows me to roll the windows down so that we can get some relief from the stifling heat that's built up in the car.

A falling star.

I think I may have made a wish that night.

In the years gone by I've tried to assign many different meanings to the experience, but so far I haven't come up with one that satisfies. There are a lot of possibilities, but nothing that I want to hang my hat on. Marjorie tells me, "It meant that you were going to be a star someday!" Yeah, well; I'm still waiting.

# An Afterword

WHY, AT SUCH a young age, was I seemingly chosen to be the recipient of so many incredible experiences, and to have a psychic gift that has enabled me to literally and accurately predict the future and have incredible insights into others' lives?

Why indeed...why was Chopin given the ability to write the Polonaise Op. 53 in A flat major and John Updike given the ability instead to write books?

Why could Horowitz come along and blister through that Polonaise in amazing fashion while I do good to play Chopsticks?

Why was Alberto Salazar born with the ability to be an incredible marathoner and I, with just as much love of running and the joy it produced for me and the yearning to be a marathoner, was born with asthma and other health conditions that kept me from ever realizing my athletic potential?

For a book that has a lot of very real problems (as all religious writings have) I do find some nuggets in the Bible, and there's one there that may perhaps explain these random assignments of gifts and talents as well as anything else:

"It is one and the same Spirit, distributing as he decides to each person, who produces all these things."

The longer I have studied and researched and explored and experienced the paranormal, the spiritual, the psychic, the more questions that I have, rather than answers.

Lord, lord...how, in all sincerity and honesty I wish I could tell you how to make more money to pay your bills, or how to communicate with your sister on the Other Side on a regular basis, or how to achieve a healing from the thing that's trying to cripple you or kill you. But I can't. And neither can anyone else. It's a pretty scary old world at its best, and that's why we need each other.

If there's a God or a Superior Intelligence or a Creator or Creators of any kind, and I believe that there is, then surely, unless this Being is some kind of morbid psychopath, its heart must hold a place for compassion to be showed forth to the universe which it has made.

And I believe that showing each other that compassion must become the highest order of business that there is for us, in our business dealings, in our friendships, in our romances, in our marriages, in our politics, in our sports: first and foremost we must strive to be helpful to one another, to love one another, to do all of the good that we can for one another.

Yes, in reasonable ways: you frequently read in the news heartbreaking stories such as the one of an elderly single woman who took a troubled young man under her wing, gave him a home with her, helped him with money and food, and he killed her one day and stole her car and took all of her money and several of her belongings that had any value. Such was the manner in which he chose to repay her kindness.

So be careful, yes. The Bible says that even Jesus didn't trust himself to man, for he knew what was in the hearts of man.

It's not all love and light out there. We have to be cautious. We do have to test the spirits to see if they speak truthfully to us or not, and we have to learn how to follow a path that's good for us and safe for us among a blather of voices that promise us the one and only way.

But I think that if we do anything, if we learn anything, if we achieve anything, it should be this, allegiance to an old Wiccan rede:

An it harm none, do what ye will.

I've traveled an awful lot of miles in my life to learn that message and to be able to share it with you through the adventures of this book. Thank you for allowing me to do so.

See you down the road.

*The End*

# Banana on My Mind

WELL...I *SAID* THE end...but this book of true ghost stories, these powerful paranormal adventures, feels far from over with for me.

For I'm sure that somewhere down the road I will have additional experiences related to my motorcycle rides, but the one I must return to, again, is Banana. After all, the guys on the Other Side told me that I would have to make repeat trips there in order to fully discover why I was called there in a dream in the first place, didn't they.

Right now Banana, and the answers that I know that it holds, are far away. And this is why.

I have had numerous serious health problems ever since I was a kid, and as I age things certainly don't get any better. And I have health issues bothering me now that rob me of energy and strength and endurance...all of the qualities requisite to mount up on Melissa and wrestle the close to 700 pounds of her metallic heft down the road.

And then there's the financial strain.

You'd think, that with all of these psychic gifts and talents, that I would be able to make myself rich, or that the Other Side would take abundant care of me financially, and yet the opposite has most often been the case. Such as it is now.

Melissa has been down for almost a full year now, languishing away in the garage, hooked up to a battery charger as she fretfully sleeps and dreams of returning to the road, and to our adventures together.

I can't afford to repair her. I've kept her running through almost 100,000 miles of adventure together, but right now I'm facing some of the tightest financial difficulties I've ever encountered and I don't have the resources to repair her in the foreseeable future, unless I were to win the lottery jackpot...and don't think that, as a psychic, I haven't tried to win that lottery jackpot, using every paranormal trick in the book that I know how to use!

Why can't I win?, I repeatedly ask the Other Side. Others do... why can't I have this money? I need to fix Melissa. I need to fix my body. It's old and worn out and sick and needs some care, and care is costly. Maintenance is expensive, whether it's a motorcycle, a car, a house, or a body.

I've resorted to bribery: Hey guys...I can't fulfill my obligation to Banana unless you help me out here financially!

I think I can hear them snickering. At least they have good senses of humor.

But I have a certainty in my heart, a faith, an assurance...I feel certain that at some point that I will be able to fix Melissa; and that I will have the energy and the strength and the endurance to saddle up once again and hit the roads, and Banana will be among our very first of destinations.

And, doggone it! When we do, if I finally discover the ultimate reason for that dream and my many return trips to old Banana, how will I tell you, my reader? How will I inform you?

I don't have a follow-up planned to this book. Will I see you at a book signing and be able to reveal Banana's ultimate secret? How will I share this with you? It's frustrating.

Well...when I finally get this book published, and I finally make my return to Banana, if I don't see you at a book signing or perhaps reach you through a radio appearance, come to my website, and if I've discovered the great Banana secret, I will tell you there.

I've enjoyed this journey with you, and I hope you've enjoyed it as well.

I'll miss you for now. Bye bye. Ride safe.

www.ridingwithghosts.net

# Poe

NO; NOT EDGAR Allen.

Over a decade ago, after my wife, Marjorie, and I had moved from New York to Florida, we went browsing. It wasn't enough that we had brought along Olivia, Sophie, and Zoe–our three cats–when we moved. We had, like most cat collectors, decided that we might need some more; especially after Olivia died.

One cheerful, bright and sunny morning, on the day that my wife was to begin her new job, Olivia was running around the house playing when we heard her give out a loud and plaintive meow. By the time we reached her she was lying on her side, legs outstretched, breathing shallowly. Our vet in New York had confirmed her heart murmur years before. She was as aghast as we were at the thought that anyone would leave behind a cherished family member pet– health reasons or not–or, god forbid, even worse: put one down. But she did warn us that the stress of the move could either do Olivia in on the drive down or cause her demise shortly thereafter, but she encouraged us to take the risk: the stress of separation from her beloved family might be worse for Olivia's heart than the trip.

Not only did Olivia survive the drive, she thrived. She was quite the trooper, and behaved better than either Zoe or Sophie, who chose to gaze out the car window from inside her carrier and vociferously protest for every single mile of the thousand mile drive. Olivia, on the other hand, actually seemed to enjoy the ride and upon reaching our new Florida home she quickly adapted to her new surroundings and lived a contented and playful life for almost a year.

But Olivia's heart gave out that morning, and as I knelt and stroked her and spoke comfortingly to her, telling her how much we loved her, she began to purr softly and made kneading motions with her paws and then, in a matter of seconds, she was gone. If you're tearing up now, it's okay: I am too.

It seems like most newspapers both large and small have begun to participate in this dastardly practice: they post the cutest pictures of cats and dogs who are available for adoption at the local shelters. Seeing the photographs of these delightful and charming animals is as addictive as crack cocaine to a pet lover: one is overcome with the urge to "score." "Just one more," we convince ourselves, "and then I'll quit. Really. I promise."

Marjorie regularly perused the photos and would often encourage me to go with her to the local shelter "Just to look." Yeah, right; we all know the axiom: if you look, you must touch, and if you touch, you must take it home with you.

Our local drug dealer (the shelter) sweetened the habit-forming offer by advertising that there had been a veritable kitten population explosion, and indeed they were not exaggerating. We went to the shelter (just to look, of course) and there was room after room full to overflowing with tiny, loveable, cute and cuddly kittens.

One *we* chose: a scowling, grumpy, menacing looking ball of fluff that we named Pandora right there on the spot. Who knew what would swim up out of that furry head of hers? Taking her home to raise would indeed be opening Pandora's box. She crouched unmoving, scowling at the other kittens that would try to engage her in play, staring coldly and menacingly at them until they averted their gazes and scampered away. "Are you sure you want *that* one?" the shelter worker asked. Yes, we did.

And then, as Marjorie herself said, one *chose us:* a noisy black ball of sleek fluff who sat close by a slightly open door and meowed nonstop until we acquiesced to his desire to own us. "Skeezix," I said, recalling a character's name from the old *Gasoline Alley* comic strip. "That's Skeezix."

We were encouraged by the shelter staff to "take more!" There were a hundred kittens or more to try and find homes for, and, "What's just one more?" We had a roomy home. We had good income so it was not a monetary strain to take care of them. But we still had Sophie and Zoe, and now with Pandora and Skeezix that would be two grown cats and two lively kittens and we politely declined adding another to our rapidly filling household.

But as we were leaving we walked by one of the glass cages and a young male cat, solid white with beautiful green eyes, caught my eye and began to talk to me through the glass, rubbing up against it as he gave me his best come-hither look. I responded by talking back to him and putting my finger against the glass as if to chuck him under his chin. "Take me home with you," he seemed to be saying, "and you won't be sorry."

"Come on," Marjorie said woefully, "I think we have enough." I had to agree, and so I waved goodbye to the white cat and we took our other charges home.

That night, while sleeping, I would suddenly and for no apparent reason pop wide awake, and each and every single time that I did so the very first thought that I became aware of was, "We have to go back and get that white cat!"

I would go back to sleep and pop wide awake again with the very same thought poking at me.

It got so bad that I began to periodically wake Marjorie up and I began to voice it aloud to her: "We have to go back and get that white cat tomorrow!"

And the next day…we did. And I named him Poe; yes, after Edgar Allen.

And oh my god. We introduced him to the kittens, Pandora and

Skeezix, and tried to feed them all together. He took one look at them, took his big old paw and soundly whacked each of them on their little heads, sending them scurrying in fright, and then calmly proceeded to dig into his food as if nothing untoward had happened. Okay...in our large home we now segregated the kittens from the grown cats.

Poe was neutered but generously sprayed a plastic trash bag that I was about to take out for garbage collection, earning a scolding from me. Had we made a mistake by bringing this rowdy guy home?

Naturally we knew nothing of his history so nothing of the state of his health either and we returned home from shopping one day to find Poe stretched out his full length on his back, lying on the couch, front legs splayed at odd and awkward angles, his back legs stretched so far that it looked to be painful as if he might have suffered some type of seizure or something, and his head cocked to the side with his eyes tightly closed and his tongue hanging far out.

"Oh my god," we whispered to each other. "Is he *dead?*"

Nope. Sleeping. So damn happy to have a home to call his own again and people that loved him that he had stretched his big old muscular frame out and *relaxed*, Poe style.

Shortly after that we learned that Poe had two modes: sound asleep; or racing around the house literally knocking over furniture.

And my god, *cat hair!* In spite of all of our grooming and brushing he would walk through a room and hair would literally fly up into the air from off of him, floating in a cloud that would eventually find its way into and onto everything. We wore out three or four vacuum cleaners because of that cat.


If you want to you can call it chauvinism, but...nature will out.

Our two grown females, Sophie and Zoe (and Olivia when she was alive), constantly bickered and fought. I've heard women who were being honest state that they hate working in an all-female office because of the bickering and fighting and that the addition of one or more men in the office will usually smooth things out somewhat.

Poe settled both Sophie and Zoe down almost immediately. He

was all male, this cat, and he walked through the house with a tough guy swagger that he could readily back up. Zoe made the mistake of challenging him; once. Never again. Sophie and Zoe would attempt to get into their little hissy fits with one another and Poe would shut it down immediately. For the first time ever peace among the cats reigned in our home.

And Poe fell absolutely totally head over heels in love with Sophie. He worshipped her. He idolized her. He made a fool of himself over her. He tried everything in his knowledge and power to gain her favorable attention, to shower her with affection, to do things for her. It was sweet, touching, and comical all at the same time. I have never seen an animal so in love with another.

Sophie, for her part, was aloof for awhile, playing hard to get and uninterested, but he finally managed to wear her down and earn her affection, although it was obvious who was most enamored between the two.

And I witnessed an amazing thing as I watched the cats interactions with each other: they would teach each other things. They began to mimic each other, and Poe introduced new behaviors that our other cats had never exhibited and they began to emulate him, and he began to mimic some of their behaviors as well. It was fascinating to watch, and an instruction in how much intelligence animals possess.

But as much as Poe loved and adored Sophie, and in a friendly manner tolerated Zoe, he never ever warmed up to Pandora or Skeezix and we had to keep them segregated until the end of days. Every chance that he got he would attack them. I never understood why.

I grew to love Poe as I had only ever loved one other cat I had known.

When I would come into the house Poe would run to greet me just as a dog would.

He loved to play, and he truly had two modes: fast asleep or racing through the house knocking things off and breaking them and overturning furniture.

He would sit in my lap and gaze adoringly into my eyes, and purr and purr as I stroked him and talked to him. He would sleep on my chest with his face close to mine.

He would respond and most times come to me when I called his name.

And, he had his quirks. As much as he loved attention, and to be stroked and petted and to lie on me or sleep with me on the couch, he hated to be picked up. He would protest loudly in an almost scared tone of voice and squirm in an attempt to get out of my arms until I put him down. It was something he never overcame, and I can only guess that it had something to do with his life before he came to us.

Another oddity of his was that he loved to come into the bathroom and bite our butts while we were sitting on the toilet. It got so bad that I finally had to close the bathroom door and keep him out, as did Marjorie, too.

I believe that he was allergic to cats. As funny as that sounds he had odd bouts of coughing and sneezing for which the vets could find no logical reason, and those bouts ended when he was the sole remaining cat in his segregated part of our home. He would also have bouts of loud wheezing, usually around the same time that I would have my own seasonal allergic and asthmatic problems.

Once I had gone into the bathroom and closed the door to avoid having my flanks repeatedly bitten by my beloved Poe. I had become a fairly tough old boy, and I had developed a fondness for the martial arts, knives, guns, and other weaponry, and an affinity for self-defense, and I usually had some type of weapon either on or near me, even in our home.

I was reading a magazine as I sat on the toilet, and from across our home I heard, coming slowly toward the bathroom door, I *swear to you* the rhythmic loud breathing of none other than *Darth Vader.* I'm not kidding. I'm not exaggerating. It got closer and louder and closer and louder and I had not a weapon one on me or near me and by God, damned if I was going to die sitting on the toilet! The horrific breathing was now right at the bathroom door and I jumped up and quickly pulled up my pants, rolled up a magazine to use as a club and jerked the door open and adopted a fighting stance, ready to attack whoever was there.

And there stood Poe, roaring in that horrible Darth Vader breathing. He coughed loudly and waddled off through the house, leaving me laughing until tears rolled down my cheeks.

Zoe died first.

Her thing was the stacks of boxes in our entry hallway that we had stopped using.

We had moved from our home in New York, which was two stories with a basement and an attic, into a one floor home and we did not get rid of anything. There are two entryways into our home from the front of our house, one through a small hallway that eventually became the repository for stacks of unpacked boxes. Our house was clean, and otherwise neat, but we had those stacks of boxes in the hallway on which Zoe loved to sleep. We could all hear her as she would wake up from a nap, shift from one box to the other, make more noise as she scooched around on it to get comfortable and then go back to sleep.

So after Zoe died she continued to give us a sign that she was still with us for awhile: me, Marjorie, and both Sophie and Poe would hear the sounds of her jumping up on those boxes, walking around and settling down for a nap. Sometimes it would be so loud that both Sophie and Poe would jump up and stare, and occasionally they would go into the hallway to investigate.

Sophie's thing was the metal water bowl. (Well, *anything* that held water. She wasn't into drinking it so much as staring into it and playing with it, and we had one of those automatic waterers with a clear plastic jug and when water would trickle down to refill the water bowl bubbles would rise up in the jug and Sophie would paw at them with such force that she would nearly knock the jug over, so we finally went to the metal water bowl.)

The metal water bowl had been a kitchen bowl at one point, and had a couple of metal rings on each side that swiveled up and down, and I presume that the rings had been used at one point to hang the bowl from hooks or to use as lifts. Not only did Sophie love to play in the water she now also developed an affinity for playing with the rings and she would flip them up with her paws so that they would clink loudly against the sides of the bowl.

After Sophie died we would all hear the loud clink of the rings as they were flipped up and down against the bowl.

(And Poe was bereft of his love, mourning for her loss like I've never seen an animal mourn.)

Poe's thing was those hollow plastic Easter eggs that come apart into two pieces. They were just about his favorite toy and he would bat them around and chase them across our tile floor all hours of the day and night.

Poe died, fittingly enough, on Halloween night. And for days afterward we would hear those plastic eggs being batted across the floor.

Sorrowfully we cleaned up the mess of cat toys and bowls, giving Pandora and Skeezix some of the surplus toys to add to their own collection. How empty the house felt with so many of our furry babies now gone. And although we still enjoyed Pandora and Skeezix, Poe was my absolute favorite little furry buddy, and my heart ached I missed him so much. I have loved a few dogs in my lifetime, deeply, but there's only one other cat I have ever loved as much as I loved Poe. His loss was irreplaceable. No one could ever match his personality and the love he showed us all.

A Halloween came and went. My sorrow at losing Poe felt as sharp as it had a year ago when he died.

Then, almost a year later, came hurricane Matthew. As we were not in the evacuation zone we obeyed the authorities directive to shelter in place in our home, which was built to hurricane standards for the state of Florida. We lost a couple of trees. One section of our fence, which borders a wild and tangled woods behind our home, was blown down, falling inward into our back yard. But thankfully our house was spared any damage.

And then we began the process of cleanup and contacting repairmen and our insurance carrier. Due to the widespread damage from Matthew it took some time before we got responses to our phone calls, much less a visit. There was so much damage to so many homes that contractors were getting hundreds and even thousands of calls, and it took time for them to process everything and get someone out to assess damage in person. In the meantime our forlorn fence lay in our yard, revealing the thicket of vines, other growth, and debris from the storm that was now our view as we gazed out into the woods through the back doors which are nearly all glass top to bottom.

One early evening only a few days before Halloween, with low sunlight still streaming into our back yard as twilight approached, Marjorie was talking on the phone as we sat on the couch watching TV. I caught movement outside in my peripheral vision and as I turned to look out the back doors a white cat was crawling, improbably, from out of the dense thicket of vines and other growth and debris, slowly making its way toward the fallen section of fence.

"Look!" I said, getting Marjorie's attention. "Look at that white cat!"

As we watched, the cat–which was the exact color and size and shape of Poe–made its way onto the fallen section of fence, sat down, and stared through the glass of our back doors, staring directly at us as we sat on the couch.

"My god, it's Poe!" I exclaimed.

We waved at the cat, who never turned his stare away from us, and I even took a picture.

"I'm going out," I said, and as I opened the door and began to call the cat it stood, turned around, and disappeared back into the thicket.

I swear, the Bible verse where Jesus tells Mary not to cling to him came to my mind, because that's what I wanted to do, was to verify that my furry little buddy Poe had come back to me and I wanted to grab him up and cling to him and hold onto him for awhile if I could.

Disappointed by the cat's disappearance I went back inside, and as Marjorie and I were discussing this visitation, once again the white cat crept back from out of the thicket onto the fence, sat, and stared at us through the glass doors while we waved to him. This time I, with difficulty, restrained myself, and simply thanked the Powers That Be and my little furry buddy Poe for the manifestation.

He sat there for a few minutes, and then crept off into the thicket in a different way from which he had come, and we've never seen him since.

Poe was a cat who left clouds of hair in the air behind him when he walked through a room. Anything he rubbed against or touched or lay on was immediately covered with his hair. And yet, in this thicket through which this cat had come, there was not a stray bit of hair to be found!

In addition Marjorie kept remarking how brilliantly glowing white he was, abnormally white, and that a cat who had made its way through all of that woodland should have been dirty. Instead he glowed whiter than white, with not a streak of dirt on him anywhere.

Odder still was the photo I took of him, for it shows a brilliant white cat sitting on the fallen fence, with no detail whatsoever…no eyes, no nose, no detail in his ears…nothing but a glowing white outline filled with shimmering white with no details at all.

It warms my heart to think that the Powers That Be would enable my buddy Poe to return, 2 years later on the anniversary of his death, for a brief visit with us, to verify that life continues after death, even for our animal friends.

It also saddens me that I couldn't have had more time with him during this visitation, but it gladdens my heart to know that I will see him again someday in the afterlife, and that maybe then I can hold him and love him once again.

I said that there had been one other cat in my life that I had loved as dearly as Poe. And he came and visited me in the flesh, too. And I actually got to touch and hold him, before he suddenly disappeared just as suddenly and as mysteriously as he had appeared.

# Gizmo

GIZMO, A TABBY cat, came into my life as a kitten. My first wife and I, with our young daughter, lived next door to a young mother and her children, and she had gotten the kitten for them, but he immediately came to our house and made himself at home.

Eventually he spent more time with us than he did with them, and I named him Gizmo after the Gremlins character. I also had a huge red female Doberman named Elsa. This gal was a rescue from the animal shelter, and I loved her more than any dog I'd ever known before. She was 100 pounds of solid muscle, sweet and smart and loving. And fascinated with Gizmo.

Gizmo would come in and either curl up in my lap, on one of the beds, or some other piece of furniture and snooze peacefully for hours. He had a sweet, friendly personality and would respond to attention with loud purrs and lots of rubbing against me. He was never destructive. He never used the bathroom in the house...we would let him outside to do his business, and thinking back (and this is so many long years ago) I don't remember if we ever purchased a litter box for him or not.

I absolutely adored the little cat, and I would pick him up and hold him in my arms, his little cheek against mine, and holding one of his paws in my hand I'd dance with him to music, or sometimes sing to him as we'd dance together. If you're a pet lover you get it. Gizmo loved that I would hold him and dance with him, and he would purr loudly and rub his face against mine as we two-stepped around the room.

Gizmo became a real-life *Garfield:* he ate so much that his little belly almost hit the floor when he sat, but in spite of becoming so chunky he was never short of energy and always ready to play. And he would eat *anything!* Doritos®; lettuce; *hot sauce.* I've never seen any other cat who would eat the variety of food that Gizmo did.

This is absolutely incomprehensible to me now, but, as many people did with their cats, we would put Gizmo out at night when we went to bed. The next day whenever he showed up from his nocturnal roaming we would let him back inside.

I say it's incomprehensible to me because at this stage of my life all of my cats have been either spayed or neutered and have spent their lives indoors. It's dangerous outside for cats: cars (Clancy, a beloved black cat from my younger days, was run over by a car.); predators; poisons; pesticides; mean people. I once read a poster at the veterinarian's office that stated that the average life expectancy for a cat that's allowed to roam outdoors is only two years!

But at the time Gizmo went out nearly every night. I think there may have been a few times where he slept in bed with us for most of the night, but not many.

If we slept late we would be awakened by a loud *bang!* on our screen door and when we opened the inner door there would be Gizmo at face height, spread-eagled like one of those toy cats with suction cups for feet that you stick to your car's window, his claws embedded in the screen, waiting for me to come outside and pluck him off of the screen door and bring him inside. That became our morning routine. Elsa, who spent the nights outside in her dog house (and all of my dogs are now inside dogs, too) would sit and stare at

Gizmo and grin at him as if she thought that was the silliest thing she'd ever seen.

I was sitting in the living room one day and Gizmo showed up at the front screen door, clawing at it furiously, trying to hook his paw underneath the door to pull it open. I got up to see why he was acting so urgently and he had with him a small black cat that was about Gizmo's age and size. I opened our door and Gizmo all but ushered the little black cat inside. He had brought home a needy friend.

So we adopted the little black cat too, naming him Pinkerton. Elsa was also fascinated with Pinkerton, but while Gizmo didn't mind her attention Pinkerton was a little bit frightened of this big red monster and remained aloof.

Gizmo was the flamboyant and dominant personality and Pinkerton seemed to gladly cede to Gizmo's status as number one cat in our household, behaving in a sedate manner and blending into the background so much that many times it was hard to realize that he was even there.

The little cats became inseparable. They never fought, but would play together and cuddle together when napping. We would put them both out at night, and when the bang on the screen door announced that Gizmo wanted in there would be Pinkerton too, sitting on the porch staring up at the door and waiting for it to open.

We loved Pinkerton too, but my heart belonged to Gizmo. Something about that furry little rascal absolutely stole my heart away, and I loved him like I had loved no other cat I had ever known.

I'll never forget it as long as I live. I've pondered the circumstances of that night over and over and I've never been able to understand it. And it hurts me to this day.

It was Thanksgiving eve night. Growing darker outside as we watched TV. Gizmo had been content in the house when all of a sudden he ran to the front screen door (it was warm enough that we had the wooden door open) and began to claw at it and push against it in a frantic manner.

I think I may have told him to just sit tight, that I'd get up and let him out in awhile, but his frantic behavior continued, and then he began to meow at me and continued to claw at the door.

"Okay, okay," I said, getting up and opening the screen door so that he could go out.

I sat back down to my TV program but I couldn't get Gizmo's odd behavior out of my mind. He had never acted that way before. It was almost like he was desperate to get out of the house. And that's the behavior I've pondered over for years and have never been able to understand, for only short moments later the neighbors came to tell me that Gizmo was lying dead in the street, having been hit by a car.

I had no cause for thanksgiving that day.

I can't tell you how hard and how long I cried at the loss of Gizmo's precious little life.

After Gizmo's unseemly and untimely death (we buried him in our yard and my daughter and I made a little cross out of Popsicle® sticks for his grave) Pinkerton's personality blossomed. Out from under Gizmo's shadow Pinkerton began to exhibit his true personality and intelligence and we were often astounded that this creative little character had been living in such a subdued manner as before.

And, idiots that we were, we continued to let Pinkerton out for the night too, until, one sad day, he never returned, and to this day I don't know what happened to him.

My wife and I divorced and Elsa came with me. I had moved back into my old family home where I had grown up, ostensibly to help my sister—who had also moved back home after her divorce—with my aging, sick and soon to be dying mother.

After our mother died I inherited the old house, and not long after my sister moved out and eventually moved to another city.

I was on the front porch one sunny weekend morning, standing on a stool while replacing a light bulb in the porch light fixture when, from around the corner of the house, this full grown but young tabby cat came racing onto the porch, meowing loudly. Tail held high he ran for my screen door and pawed at it, much as Gizmo had done when he was alive.

This young cat was the spitting image of Gizmo if he had grown into an adult, and all I could do for a moment was stand on the stool and stare, open-mouthed.

*"Gizmo?"* I asked the cat.

I got down from the stool and gave him some strokes to which he responded by purring loudly. I opened the door and he raced into my house, meowing happily and continuing to purr loudly.

I was so astounded that I didn't quite know how to act.

About that time the washing machine announced that it was done with my load of clothes, so, while this cat rubbed all around my legs I placed the wet clothes into my clothes basket and, as I didn't have a dryer, I took them outside to hang on the clotheslines that my parents had erected when they had bought the house many years ago.

The cat followed me out into the back yard and leapt up at the clothes basket as I carried it, rubbing himself against it midair. He seemed to be so overjoyed to see me, to be with me.

Elsa, who was in her large outdoor pen, caught sight of the cat and gave out a bark that was almost a yelp.

When the cat spied her he ran to her pen and began to wallow all over the sidewalk directly in front of the gate that opened into her enclosure. She hunkered down and pawed at the cat, and I swear it was if they recognized each other and were having a reunion!

I shook my head, finished hanging my clothes up on the clotheslines, and after I carried the empty clothes basket back inside my house in stereotypical fashion of the day I poured a saucer of milk to bring outside to the cat, who had been frolicking with Elsa when last I saw him.

I sat the saucer of milk down on the back porch, called, "Here, kitty kitty kitty kitty kitty," and looked around the corner of the house toward Elsa's pen.

The cat was gone; disappeared. And I never saw it again.

But I sure hope that I get to see, and hold and love, all of the precious pets that have passed away over the years, and I'm especially grateful for the visitation from Gizmo, and many years later, from Poe.

Now, if Elsa would just come and see me.

# Afterword: The Haunted Camera

A DEAR FAMILY friend who I will refer to as Frank, my mother, and myself were holding a mediumistic circle, an intimate séance, if you will. The Vivitar XV-2 camera was introduced in approximately 1978–the body retailing for $100–which is about when I must have bought mine from Nathan's Jewelers in San Angelo, TX. At this juncture I had owned the camera for well over a decade, possibly as long as 15 years. The camera took great, sharp photos and had always functioned flawlessly. I had loaded the Vivitar with a fresh roll of film, intending to take some spirit photos.

During the circle all of us discerned the spirit of a woman present, and we all gave the same matching description of her, down to intimate details about her physical appearance, the way in which she was dressed, etc.

I announced that I wanted to attempt to take a spirit photograph of her and readied my camera. Both Frank and my mother said that the spirit didn't want to be photographed. I was determined, and I announced that I was going to attempt to take her photo and I asked her to please manifest on film for me. Frank and my mother kept saying, "John, she doesn't want you to take her photo." I persisted, and something impossible happened.

I pressed the shutter release button, there was the clearly audible sound of the shutter clicking open and closed, and then I activated the film advance lever, watching as the film rewind knob spun to indicate that the film was advancing...except that I could tell that the film did not advance!

I attempted another shot, in spite of their continued warnings, and the exact same thing happened. I opened the camera back in subdued light, made a note of the frame number, closed the camera and attempted another shot. Again the noise of the shutter click, I pressed the film advance lever, the film rewind knob spun to indicate that the film was advancing, and yet when I opened the camera back and checked again the film was still on the exact same frame number!

Another few shots produced the same results, with the physical impossibility of the film rewind knob spinning as I pressed the film advance lever while the same frame of film remained in place. A literal physical impossibility. The only way for the film rewind knob to spin is for the film to have advanced in the camera.

I laughed and said, "Okay, I get the message. I'm sorry I tried to take a photo of you when you didn't want me to."

Immediately Frank said, "Try it now. It will work now!"

I did, and when I checked the film it had indeed advanced!

I proceeded to take the rest of the roll (with the exposure counter showing more frames than what the roll of film contained as it counted each stroke of the film advance lever) and that's when things really got weird.

When the film was developed there was a jumble of unrecognizable multiple exposures on that one frame of film that had momentarily frozen in time.

In one of the shots there were three clearly visible little "comets" that were weaving in and out among the arms of a lampstand, but that was the only evidence we got that a spirit, or spirits, had been involved...with the exception of what happened to my camera.

The camera that had worked flawlessly still did...except that without explanation some shots on the same roll of film would be hopelessly blurry, or overexposed to the point of almost being whited out, underexposed almost to the point of the print being black, and sometimes odd looking photos occurred that looked like multiple exposures.

Then it really got bizarre.

My camera began to leak oil. To *drip* oil! If I sat the camera down on a surface and then picked it up I would have to wipe up the oil that had leaked out of it. The inside of the camera became saturated with oil, and the phenomenon would reoccur in spite of my regularly wiping the inside dry with a cloth or paper towels. It got so bad that there was no way to load the camera with film any longer and utilize it for photos.

Then the shutter stopped working. Then, inexplicably, the film advance lever froze. And finally the letters and numbers visible in the exposure counter window all rotated out of view and disappeared.

The camera has never worked again to this day; the manifestation of the leaking oil did, however, finally stop.

I guess that woman in spirit really did not want me to attempt to take her photograph.

CPSIA information can be obtained
at www.ICGtesting.com
Printed in the USA
LVHW080950170321
681751LV00011B/125